SO-ADK-253

FROM BELOW:

INDEPENDENT PEACE AND ENVIRONMENTAL MOVEMENTS

IN EASTERN EUROPE AND THE USSR

OCTOBER 1987

A HELSINKI WATCH REPORT

36 W. 44th Street
New York, NY 10036
212-840-9460

739 Eighth Street, S.E.
Washington, DC 20003
202-546-9336

U.S. HELSINKI WATCH COMMITTEE

The U.S. Helsinki Watch Committee was founded in 1979 to promote domestic and international compliance with the human rights provisions of the 1975 Helsinki accords. Its Chairman is Robert L. Bernstein; its Vice Chairman is Aryeh Neier; its Executive Director is Jeri Laber; its Washington Representative is Holly Burkhalter.

(c)   1987 by The Helsinki Watch Committee
All rights reserved
Printed in the United States of America
ISBN 0-938579-67-3

Bound copies are available for $12.00.

TABLE OF CONTENTS

ACKNOWLEDGMENTS

This report was written by Catherine Fitzpatrick and Janet Fleischman, with the assistance of Stanley Engelstein and Brian Barrett on the East German chapter, Marta Toch on the Polish chapter, and Vladimir Mijanovic and Bojana Mladenovic on the Yugoslav chapter. The report is based on an article by Catherine Fitzpatrick that appeared in <u>Sojourners</u> in February 1987 entitled, "Into The Public Eye: The Emergence of Independent Peace Movements in the Soviet bloc." Helsinki Watch is grateful for the editorial assistance of A. Winton Jackson, editor of <u>Across Frontiers</u>, and John Glusman, member of the Helsinki Watch Committee, in addition to the insights provided by Joanne Landy of the Campaign for Peace and Democracy/East and West and Pat Hunt of European Nuclear Disarmament.

INTRODUCTION

One of the most exciting developments of the 1980s in Eastern Europe and the Soviet Union has been the emergence of independent citizens' peace and ecology movements, coupled with a widening discussion about disarmament, militarism and ecology among the civil rights movements that were launched in the 1960s and 1970s. Although the human rights and other social movements of the East European countries are very different in nature, they all have a common desire to reclaim from the state what is called "civil society" in the languages of these countries, or what might be called "public life" or "community activism" in the West.

The notion of "civil society" implies a space where independent discussion and criticism can grow, where an alternative to the state's monopoly on information and education can thrive, where an effort can be made to restrain the state's arbitrary or arrogant use of power against its own citizens or other countries and, finally, where the rigidity and isolation of the bloc mentality can be challenged. Activists in Eastern Europe have described this process as restoring the citizens as a subject of history, rather than as an object controlled by the state.

The success of this struggle has differed from country to country. But in all of the Soviet bloc states and Yugoslavia, independent peace and human rights activity has been met with harsh retaliation from the security forces, which regard any unofficial citizens' initiatives as a challenge to their authority and power.

Four major events in the last decade have dramatically

1

altered the stage and the players in Eastern Europe and expanded the space for "public life." The first grew out of the signing of the Helsinki Final Act on Security and Cooperation in Europe 12 years ago by 35 nations, including the United States and the Soviet Union. The Helsinki accords are not legally binding, but they are part of a continuing process of establishing security in Europe and improving trade and human rights conditions.

The signatories agreed to ratify the post World War II borders in Europe and to refrain from seeking to change them by force, as well as from interfering in one another's internal affairs. This was of paramount importance to the security-conscious Soviet Union, both a victim and a perpetrator of many invasions in its purported quest for national security. But the accords also provided a new, public acknowledgment to the peoples of Eastern Europe of their governments' commitments to internationally accepted human rights standards and proclaimed the indissoluble link between human rights and peace. This gave the Western democracies leverage in pushing for an opening in the closed societies of the East.

The Helsinki accords emphasize the free flow of information and people, addressing the West's concern that the repressive nature of East bloc governments causes suffering to citizens and is a threat to international security since preparations for war in these countries are cloaked in secrecy and remain beyond public control. The accords sparked citizens' "watch" committees and public petitioning in the Soviet bloc and continue to be a basis for all peace and human rights activity today.

The second major event was the growth of Solidarity, the free trade union and democracy movement in Poland which, at its height, was 10 million strong. Solidarity continues to transform Polish life and is the largest independent social movement in Eastern Europe. In an unprecedented development, this mass movement was able to force an agreement with the government that was observed for a year and a half before the imposition of martial law in December 1981.

This agreement enabled the public to create its own institutions so that even the judiciary was reformed and police abuse curbed. Independent publications flourished and continue to this day, and participation in independent cultural activities is still widespread. An outgrowth of detente that probably would not have been possible without the signing of the Helsinki accords, the Solidarity movement spilled over into all the neighboring states of the East.

The third major influence on Eastern European social movements was the appearance of a vigorous Western peace movement, which flourished in Europe particularly during the period 1980-1984. The mass movements against nuclear weapons in Western Europe evoked an interest in the same issues in Eastern Europe, where citizens feel tied by history and fate to their West European counterparts and where independent proposals have also been made on disarmament, the creation of nuclear-free zones, the withdrawal of all foreign troops and a dissolution of the East-West bloc system itself. Conscientious objection has been particularly attractive to young people in the East who are subject to compulsory military education and the draft.

The fourth major event of the 1980s was the nuclear disaster in Chernobyl in May 1986, which provoked a tide of fear and indignation among the peoples of Eastern Europe who were in the path of the radioactive cloud. Demonstrations and protests of one kind or another occurred in almost all of the Soviet bloc countries. Calls to abolish nuclear power began to be heard, and the "green" or ecological movement gained impetus.

These independent peace and environmental initiatives in the East differ from similar Western movements, mainly because official oppression has inhibited their work and because some major differences in perspective on the link between peace and human rights have grown out of these countries' specific experiences under Soviet oppression. But all the groups have reached out to their Western counterparts, despite some disagreements. Were it not for support for these groups by major Western peace organizations, they would have been crushed by state security agencies long ago.

The following is a summary of recent activities stemming from major peace and environmental initiatives in Czechoslovakia, East Germany, Hungary, Poland, the USSR and Yugoslavia.

Catherine Fitzpatrick
Research Director
September 1987

I. CZECHOSLOVAKIA

No evil has ever been eliminated by suppressing its symptoms. We need to address the cause itself. -- Vaclav Havel, <u>Politics and Conscience</u>.

Soviet-led Warsaw Pact troops invaded Czechoslovakia in 1968 to put down what is known as the "Prague Spring," a reform movement that sought "socialism with a human face." Hundreds of thousands of people were imprisoned or fired from their jobs in the aftermath of the invasion; many of these individuals form the basis for the independent movements of today.

There are currently 80,000 Soviet troops stationed in Czechoslovakia, exerting a chilling effect on developments in a country whose political system has remained virtually unchanged since 1968. Repression remains severe for anyone who challenges official policies. Nevertheless, an active and committed human rights community continues to exist, largely centered around Charter 77.

Charter 77 is both a civil rights movement and a manifesto which was issued by Czechoslovak intellectuals and workers in January 1977 seeking the Czechoslovak government's compliance with the Helsinki accords. In the ten years of its existence -- longer than any other human rights group has survived in Eastern Europe -- more than 1,300 people have signed the Charter, and it has spawned a wealth of cultural, publishing, human rights, peace and ecological activities. Charter 77 has also issued an impressive array of independent documentation on human rights abuse, law, environmental pollution, religion and other issues. The movement's structure and aims are best described in its founding declaration:

> Charter 77 is not an organization; it has no rules,
> permanent bodies or formal membership. It embraces
> everyone who agrees with its ideas, participates in its
> work, and supports it. It does not form the basis for
> any oppositional political activity. Like many similar
> citizen initiatives in various countries, West and East,
> it seeks to promote the general public interest. It does
> not aim, then, to set out its own programs for
> political or social reforms or changes, but within its
> own sphere of activity it wishes to conduct a
> constructive dialogue with the political and state
> authorities, particularly by drawing attention to
> various individual cases where human and civil rights
> are violated, by preparing documentation and
> suggesting solutions, by submitting other proposals of
> a more general character aimed at reinforcing such
> rights and their guarantees, and by acting as a
> mediator in various conflict situations which may lead
> to injustice and so forth.[1]

Peace Issues

Though no independent peace movement exists as such in
Czechoslovakia, a variety of discussions on peace have been
carried out under the auspices of Charter 77 and, in June 1987,
Charter 77 set up a working group on peace (see p. 17). A major
priority for Charter 77 has been to maintain an ongoing dialogue
with Western peace movements. Most independent peace groups

in Eastern Europe, notably those in Poland and East Germany, have acknowledged the important role that Charter has played in the evolution of their own movements by so aptly articulating the position that peace and human rights are inextricably intertwined. Many observers believe that the best theoretical writing on the relationship between peace and human rights has come from Charter 77 and from individual Chartists.

That is not to say that all independent peace activity in Czechoslovakia has originated with the Chartists. Separate and spontaneous peace activities -- particularly in 1983 at the time of Soviet missile deployment in Czechoslovakia -- have included the following: petitions protesting deployment of Soviet missiles in 1983, with some 2,000 signatories, that originated with workers in Moravia; a 1983 campaign against deployment using the sun as a symbol, begun by university students who painted suns on university boards, posters and stickers; and young people tagging on to an official peace march in 1983. More recent examples include the emergence of the "Lennonists" and Young Art for Peace (see below).

As early as November 1981, Charter 77 issued documents emphasizing "the indivisibility of peace and freedom" and expressing its positive attitude toward the Western peace movement.[2] In a March 1982 open letter to the peace movements, Charter elaborated its position as follows: "To guarantee peace it is necessary to eliminate violence and injustice within states and guarantee respect by the state authorities in all countries of human and civil rights...We feel we cannot believe the genuineness of peace efforts where fundamental human and civil rights are suppressed..." The document recognizes the exceptional threat posed by nuclear war, but states that "it is solely in relation to all other human rights that peace is not what it can become, namely a temporary strategy of the powerful or a naive demand of those who wish to protect life at all cost, regardless of human responsibility to the values which surpass life itself." According to Charter, the urgency of the peace issue and the suspect manner in which governmental authorities have coopted the peace issue for their own political purposes demands that peace issues be dealt with by "unofficial action by ordinary citizens."[3]

A watershed in the East-West peace discussion came in the form of a letter written in April 1983 by Jaroslav Sabata, a Charter 77 signatory and former spokesperson, addressed to E.P. Thompson, a British historian and leader of European Nuclear Disarmament (END). Among other things, Sabata discusses the necessity of an alternative to both peaceful coexistence and nuclear annihilation; namely, a "democratic peace." "Any grassroots peace activity in whatever part of Europe," he claims, "will lose its identity and cease to be autonomous if it fails to develop in the spirit of such a major democratic transformation." With regard to disarmament negotiations, Sabata notes that "to propose a Pact on the non-use of armed force and the maintenance of peaceful relations while refusing peaceful relations and a dialogue with one's own people (and indeed sending them to prison for holding contrary views) means proposing a signature on a worthless piece of paper."[4] Sabata's notion of a democratic peace, which implies that peace is not simply the absence of weapons but also the absence of political and social tensions, has become an accepted term in the peace movement and has had a direct impact on an important section of the West European peace movement's interpretation of the peace issue.

In June 1983, the World Assembly for Peace and Life Against Nuclear War -- organized by the Soviet-dominated World Peace Council -- was held in Prague. A formal request by Charter 77 to participate in the Assembly, which was allegedly open to all movements defending peace, was rejected by the authorities. Prior to the opening of the Assembly, numerous Charter signatories were interrogated and threatened with arrest if they tried to contact delegates to the Assembly or Western journalists covering the event. This resulted in the following:

o   Friends of Ladislav Lis, a key figure in the dialogue between Charter 77 and the Western peace movement who was in prison at the time of the Assembly, were warned that if they tried to associate Lis's case with the peace movement or to provide information about him to foreign journalists, they would be prosecuted under Article 112 (harming the interests of the Republic abroad).

o   On June 23, Charter representatives met separately with 20 West European activists in a city park, where a statement of cooperation was drawn up. Secret police photographed the meeting and seized the film of Western reporters.

o   The organizations Greenpeace and Pax Christi International withdrew their delegates from the Assembly because of the harassment of Charter activists. Delegates representing the West German "Greens" left the conference, protesting "violent attacks" against press freedom and freedom of expression.

o   During the Congress, five Czech youths were arrested

after a group of 200 broke away from a large official
peace march, chanting their own slogan, "We want peace
and freedom." Several young workers were detained for
circulating petitions against the deployment of Soviet
missiles.

It should also be noted that the Jazz Section -- which carried
out one of the most innovative and successful efforts at
spreading independent culture in Czechoslovakia until the arrest
of its leadership in September 1986 -- distributed a statement at
the Congress. In addressing the connection between jazz music
and world peace, the Jazz Section stated:

> Our organization represents several thousand
> people from the whole country who are interested in
> modern music. The word jazz is more than a label
> for a certain kind of music; it stands for a symbol of
> creativity, humanity and tolerance. We consider
> music as a universal language, as a way to mutual
> understanding both between people and nations. We
> believe people searching spontaneously for a common
> language are as important for peace as professional
> diplomats negotiating at disarmament conferences.
>   We are convinced that war cannot be averted by
> mere declarations. War can only be avoided under
> one condition: people must *want* to live in peace.
> They must realize that war means not only loss of life
> and material damage, but also an irreparable
> catastrophe of culture, which warps the characters and
> moral values of those who survive....Peace gives music

all possibilities for further development -- war needs
only brass military marches.[5]

After the Soviets deployed short-range missiles in
Czechoslovakia in October 1983, the authorities threatened some
20 Charter activists with imprisonment on charges of
undermining the country's national defense capability if they
criticized the stationing of Soviet missiles in Czechoslovakia.
Charter appealed to the government "to allow citizens the right to
express themselves freely on all matters of public interest" and
expressed concern over the escalation of the arms race and the
deployment of nuclear missiles on Czechoslovak territory.[6]

Charter 77 was instrumental in initiating joint statements
among independent movements in Eastern Europe. Members of
Charter 77 and KOR (Workers' Defense Committee in Poland)
first met in August 1978 on the 10th anniversary of the invasion
of Czechoslovakia and issued a joint statement.[7] In 1984,
Charter was involved in a number of joint statements, including:
a February 1984 joint Czechoslovak-Polish appeal protesting the
imprisonment of Charter signatories, members of KOR and
activists of Solidarity and pledging to "struggle for the
observation of human rights and civil freedoms;"[8] a July 1984
statement by Charter 77 and independent Hungarian peace
activists; and a November 1984 declaration signed by Charter and
independent East German peace activists, protesting the
stationing of Soviet missiles in their countries and expressing
their solidarity with the Western peace movements.[9] All these
statements incorporated Charter's position on the links between
peace and human rights and, as such, reflect the influence that
Charter has had on movements in other countries.

The joint statements also indicated the beginning of a logistically difficult but extremely productive dialogue among independent groups in Eastern Europe. What began with efforts at East-West communication, as evidenced by Charter's early dialogue with the Western peace movement, turned to the far more difficult task of developing some East-East communication. This contributed to the development of a truly East-West dialogue, the most recent and significant example of which was the November 1986 memorandum addressed to the CSCE Review Conference in Vienna entitled, "Giving Real Life to the Helsinki Accords" (see Appendix VI). Charters' role has been integral to this process.

In many respects, the Helsinki memorandum was stimulated by a March 1985 statement issued by a group of Chartists, known as the "Prague Appeal." Though not a Charter document, the appeal is a general consensus statement on peace that was addressed to the July 1985 END convention in Amsterdam and called for responses from Eastern and Western groups. It is important to note that the Prague Appeal was the first document to link peace issues with the Helsinki process; it led the Western peace movements to pay more attention to the Helsinki accords as a framework within which the peace issue could be approached. The Prague Appeal states (for full text, see Appendix I):

> The Conference on Security and Cooperation in Europe and its Final Act signed in Helsinki are...not just an acknowledgment of the status quo, but also constitute a program of European and Euro-American cooperation....The requirement that governments

12

should fulfill all their undertakings and obligations has not been made full use of by the peace movement.

A democratic and sovereign Europe is inconceivable so long as any of its citizens, groups of citizens or nations are denied the right to take part in decisions affecting not only their everyday lives but their very survival. Within a framework of cooperation and dialogue among all those who genuinely seek to overcome the present dangerous situation, it should be possible to come forward with different disarmament initiatives and proposals...In short, it is necessary to support all actions by individuals, groups and governments seeking the rapprochement and free association of European nations while rejecting any measures which might postpone or thwart the achievement of this ideal....The freedom and dignity of citizens are the key to the freedom and self-determination of nations. And only sovereign nations can transform Europe into a community of equal partners which would not pose the threat of a global nuclear war, but instead serve as an example of real peaceful coexistence.[10]

The responses to the Prague Appeal from individuals and groups of the East and of the West representing over 20 countries -- including most of Western Europe in addition to East Germany, Hungary and Poland -- were published and distributed by Charter. Though the signatories of the Prague Appeal never formally addressed the responses, many of the comments and criticisms submitted were taken up in subsequent Charter

13

documents.[11]

Czech youths have also been vocal in the call for peace. On May 26, 1986, a group of young people requested official permission to establish an organization, "Young Art for Peace." The idea of the organization was to work for peace within the framework of the National Front. In requesting the approval of its by-laws, submitted to the Ministry of the Interior, the group stated:

> ...We are advocates of peace and the disarmament of the whole world. We do not want only to criticize, point out mistakes and shortages, protest against existing facts -- yet do nothing about it. We want to search for assistance, which would help to correct the complex problems. Art has the capacity to cross over this abyss. It is able to "wipe out" frontiers between nations and helps people to "come together"... We want to organize this activity within the framework of the National Front and thus assist further development of our country and the whole world...[12]

Between 500-700 young people signed a petition in support of this request. The security police, however, responded with a variety of threats, including loss of employment, dismissal from institutions of higher learning, criminal prosecution and other forms of harassment. On July 5, the security police forced the organization to withdraw its request. During interrogations, the police called the young people "the young blood of Charter 77," claiming that Charter 77 was acting as an advisor to them.[13] There were no formal links between Charter and the Young Art for Peace, but the young people were undoubtedly influenced by

14

Charter's documents, especially those on youth and peace, and there were indirect relations between some Chartists and the young people. Nevertheless, none of the members of Young Art were Charter signatories.

Other peace actions included:

o   Six people were sentenced on April 28, 1986, to jail terms of up to 20 months for taking part in a poster campaign against Soviet missiles and Soviet influence in Czechoslovakia. Dalibor Helstyn, a worker, received the highest sentence: 20 months of imprisonment in the first prison category, unconditionally, and a fine of 5,000 crowns (about two months' salary) or two additional months of imprisonment. Helstyn was charged under Article 100/1/a (incitement) of the Criminal Code and under Article 136 (damage caused to property in socialist ownership). Helstyn allegedly stated that he wanted to express, through his slogans, his disagreement with the policy of culture of the socialist system, that Lenin's theory on socialist revolution should be implemented in a different form, and that in his view, there is no difference between the armaments of the socialist and capitalist countries.[14]

Another form of spontaneous peace activity in Czechoslovakia involves young people who have taken John Lennon as a symbol. Every December, on the anniversary of Lennon's death, hundreds of young people congregate at the "Lennon Wall" (formerly the "wall of democracy") on Kampa island in Prague, chanting peace slogans and writing poems on the wall.[15] Those participating in the demonstration are often subjected to interrogation and house searches by the police. In the 1982-1984 demonstrations, clashes with the police were quite severe.

o   On December 8, 1985, the fifth anniversary of the John Lennon's assassination, over 600 young people from different parts of Czechoslovakia demonstrated in Prague. During the procession, which took the demonstrators through many parts of the city, slogans were chanted such as: "We want freedom, we want peace;" "Do away with SS20s;" "Do away with the army;" etc. The crowd was dispersed by police and one of the organizers was taken away for questioning.[16]

Reports indicate that there are over 1,000 "Lennonists" in Czechoslovakia, but precise numbers are difficult to estimate; they organize locally and focus their activities on ecological concerns, music (distributing cassettes, etc.) and peace issues (calling for the withdrawal of Soviet troops and missiles, a reduction in length of military service to one year, and the right to conscientious objection).

In March 1986, Charter issued a document demanding "space for Czechoslovak youth," which discussed spontaneous peace and musical activities organized by Czechoslovak young people. In addition to calling for unrestricted travel for young people, Charter proposed a reduction in the length of compulsory military service from 24 months to 18 months and an introduction of the right to conscientious objection. "Society could make good use of this service without weapons," the

16

document stated, "particularly in the field of forestry conservation and the protection of the environment in general, as well as in the care of the aged and disabled."[17]

In October 1986, on the occasion of the Peace Congress in Copenhagen, Charter issued a statement outlining the efforts it had undertaken, notably since 1981, with regard to the link between peace and human rights. Significantly, the statement also discusses other forms of spontaneous peace activity in Czechoslovakia, including the pilgrimage to Velehrad for the anniversary of the death of St. Methodius, various petition campaigns against deployment of Soviet missiles, the Lennonists' demonstration in 1985, Young Art for Peace and the activities of the Jazz Section. Charter asked that the Congress "show interest in these spontaneous expressions, which are an authentic effort for the cause of peace."

> Peace is not threatened only where new offensive weapons are being manufactured. Peace is threatened everywhere, where the voice of the critically thinking citizen has been silenced. It is therefore foolish to think that peace efforts can be limited only to military-technical aspects of disarmament and that the problem of human rights and freedom be left to organizations such as Amnesty International....Real peace does not mean only the removal of despotism from relations among states, but also from relations between state power and a human being.[18]

As mentioned above, in June 1987 Charter formed a separate working group to deal with the peace issue. The working group, which was created in the aftermath of the Freedom and Peace seminar in Warsaw in May 1987 (see Chapter IV, Poland), proposed to work "on questions of peace and their connection with human and civic rights, as well as on demands concerning the observance of civic rights in the army during compulsory service."[19]

Another interesting initiative was announced in a letter by Charter 77 to the END convention in Coventry, England, in July 1987. Charter announced that it would hold a peace seminar in Prague, hopefully in the winter or spring of 1988. According to Charter, such a seminar would enable the East-West dialogue to go beyond an exchange of letters to a true discussion and would "be a valuable test of the quality of our political thinking and also living proof of detente and new political thinking in practice." [20]

Environmental Issues

The ecological crisis that is facing Czechoslovakia -- and the rest of Eastern Europe -- has become so severe that the government has been forced to address the issue. However, as is the case with the peace issue, independent views and public debate are not permitted. Charter first established a working group on the environment in 1978. Since then, it has been the primary source for independent information about the environment, though various ecological actions have been undertaken by other quarters of society, notably young people.

Andrew Csepel, writing in East European Reporter, explained why the authorities had been forced to release at least some information on the ecological crisis: "The chief reason why the Party has ceased to ignore [the environmental issue] is quite simply that the environment is a visible catastrophe, threatening the foundations of industrial and agricultural production, not to mention the nation's health."[21] He goes on to discuss a report on the situation that was commissioned by the Czechoslovak Academy of Sciences in late 1981 or early 1982 which deals primarily with acid rain, the chemicalization of agriculture and water pollution. The report, however, made no mention of nuclear energy.

In all areas, but particularly with regard to the pollution of water supplies, the report's conclusions are grim: 45-60 percent of Czechoslovakia's forests will be destroyed by pollution by the year 2000; the problem of acid rain is extremely serious, particularly in the Czech Republic; and contaminated drinking water has led to epidemics of diseases such as typhoid and dysentery.[22]

Environmental dangers have also led to some cooperation among independent movements in the East bloc. The Danube Circle, for example, an independent Hungarian group fighting construction of a joint Hungarian-Czechoslovak hydro-electric dam at Gabcikovo-Nagymaros (see Chapter III, Hungary), approached Charter 77 to appeal to the Czechoslovak public regarding the environmental consequences of the project. In September 1985, Charter issued an appeal to the state authorities to re-examine the project and released the text of the Danube Circle's appeal to the Czechoslovak public which stated:

The hysterical industrialization of the 1950s and the continuous plundering of the economy have caused irreversible damage in many regions of

Bohemia, Moravia, Slovakia and Hungary. The construction of the planned hydro-electric barrage system at Gabcikovo-Nagymaros is likely to have irreversible consequences which will affect all the nations living along the Danube....We appeal to the Czechoslovak public to join us in our fight to defend ecological values and the Danube region.[23]

The official press coverage of the Chernobyl accident in the Soviet Union was generally poor. In May 1986, Charter 77 issued a document addressed to the Federal Assembly of Czechoslovakia which discussed the government's inadequate response to the crisis. According to Charter, the government issued two statements -- on April 30 and on May 5 -- which provided practically no information on radioactive levels in the country and no information on medical measures that should be taken. The Charter document stated:

> As the right to life and health belongs to basic human rights, we demand that you publish as soon as possible all available facts concerning if and on what level there was increased radioactivity during the individual days of the critical period on the territory of our country. Especially important is to publish the unembellished opinions of experts who should tell the public what risks still exist and what measures it is necessary to implement immediately and in the future.[24]

In its first document of 1987, "A Word to our Fellow

Citizens," Charter raised the ecological crisis and saw the government's attitude toward it as one of the primary problems facing the country. "We all know how catastrophic the ecological situation is in our country. Why do we talk about it only in private? Why do we talk in public about only one-tenth of these problems?...We should open, in various settings and on all levels, a basic discussion about the ecological situation here." [25]

On April 30, 1987, Charter issued document 33/87, "Let the People Breathe." The 12-page document, which was sent to several government agencies, concentrates on air pollution caused by industry in Czechoslovakia. Its demands include the installation of filter equipment in plants using coal and the use of technological improvements to save energy and discusses the dangers posed by nuclear power plants.[26] The Charter study states:

> In this text, we have dealt with the pollution of the atmosphere. This does not mean to imply that the state of surface and underground water is any less alarming. However, that specific problem will be the subject of a future Charter 77 document. Even so, we feel that the above text entitles us to state that what we are facing is not just an economic and ecological problem. This is a major, fundamental moral problem: In what condition will we hand over this country to future generations?[27]

On June 10, 1987, Charter held its first "forum" in Prague, a new initiative designed to stimulate independent discussion and activity in Czechoslovakia. The fact that Charter was able to conduct the forum -- which was attended by some 50 people including foreign journalists -- without police interference is highly significant. The theme of the forum was ecology, and Charter's April document provided the basis for much of the discussion. Reports indicate that a number of suggestions were put forth designed to deal with the growing crisis.

As a result of the forum, an organizing committee was formed, comprised of both Charter signatories and environmental activists. The committee will investigate possibilities for implementing some of the suggestions and proposals that were raised at the forum.

Notes -- Czechoslovakia

[1] Reprinted in Gordon H. Skilling, Charter 77 and Human Rights in Czechoslovakia. London: George Allen & Unwin, 1981.

[2] "Statement on West European Peace Movements," November 15, 1981. Reprinted in Voices From Prague: Documents on Czechoslovakia and the Peace Movement, edited by Jan Kavan and Zdena Tomin. London: Palach Press Ltd., 1983.

[3] "Open Letter to Peace Movements," March 29, 1982, Voices from Prague, op. cit.

[4] "Letter to E.P. Thompson," April 1983, Voices from Prague, op. cit.

[5] "Jazz Section Suppressed," END Journal, #25, December 1986-January 1987.

[6] Radio Free Europe Bulletin, December 12, 1983.

[7] Jan Josef Lipski, KOR Workers' Defense Committee in Poland, 1976-81. Los Angeles: University of California Press, 1985.

[8] Palach Press Summary of Available Documents #24, April 1984, p. 66.

[9] Palach Press Summary of Available Documents #25,

December 1984, p. 37.

[10] Reprinted in Campaign for Peace & Democracy East/West, Peace & Democracy News, New York: Summer-Fall 1985.

[11] Jan Kavan, Palach Press.

[12] Anna Faltus, Czechoslovak National Council of America, August 24, 1986.

[13] Ibid.

[14] Anna Faltus, op. cit., May 24, 1986.

[15] Jan Kavan, "Spontaneous Peace Demo in Prague," East European Reporter,Vol. 1 No. 4, Winter 1986.

[16] Ibid.

[17] "Charter 77 Demands Space for Czechoslovak Youth, East European Reporter, Vol. 2 No. 1, Spring 1986.

[18] Faltus, Oct. 24, 1986.

[19] Faltus, Charter 77 document #40/87, July 16, 1987.

[20] Jan Kavan, Palach Press.

[21] Andrew Csepel, "Marxism and the Ecological Crisis, East European Reporter, Summer 1985.

[22] Palach Press, <u>Summary of Available Documents</u>, July 1984.

[23] Palach Press, <u>op. cit.</u>, October 1985.

[24] Faltus, Charter 77 document # 15/86, May 6, 1986.

[25] Faltus, January 1, 1987.

[26] <u>Foreign Broadcast Information Service</u>, June 22, 1987.

[27] <u>East European Reporter</u>, Vol. 2, #4.

II. EAST GERMANY (GERMAN DEMOCRATIC REPUBLIC)

If therefore we want to remain alive--away with the weapons! And first of all: away with the nuclear weapons....We propose that the great debate about questions of peace be conducted in an atmosphere of tolerance and recognition of the right of free expression, and that every spontaneous public manifestation of the desire for peace should be approved and encouraged.

From the Berlin Appeal, "Make Peace Without Weapons," January 1982.

The GDR has the highest standard of living among the Eastern bloc states and has special relations with West Germany. Nevertheless, 380,000 Soviet troops are stationed in the GDR, and the country remains firmly within the Soviet orbit. The Berlin Wall -- erected in 1961 -- is the symbol and reality of the division of Europe, designed to stem the tide of thousands of East Germans who sought to flee the country. Despite a heavily mined border, dozens of people try to cross over to West Germany each year; many die in the attempt.

Since 1961, some 268,000 people, largely retired persons, have been allowed to emigrate; another 190,000 have attempted to leave without authorization; 182 cases have been documented of persons killed while trying to escape over the Wall; 60,000 have been arrested and charged for trying to escape and about 5,000 who attempted to flee are being held in prison at this time. The West German government is believed to have spent millions of dollars to buy freedom for thousands of East Germans.

East German citizens have more contact with Western Europe than other Soviet bloc citizens; they watch West German television and receive visits from West German relatives -- more than 40,000 a year. Western peace movements and demonstrations are given extensive coverage in the East German media. Recently, it was announced that travel restrictions will be eased slightly to allow more East Germans to travel to West Germany. At one point, in 1982-83, the autonomous peace movement in East Germany was one of the largest in Eastern Europe, capable of turning out large numbers of participants at events organized independently of the state. The GDR movement, which became identified by the slogan "Swords Into Plowshares," engendered various other groups such as Women For Peace which sought alternative military service and the abolishment of the sale of war toys, and protested both NATO and Warsaw Pact missile deployment and troop presence.

Peace Activity

Autonomous peace activity caught the public eye in East Germany after 1981, largely stimulated by the presence of a mass disarmament movement in West Germany, by the growing militarization of East German society, and by NATO and Warsaw Pact deployment of medium-range nuclear missiles in Europe. Under the protection of the church, the independent peace movement has developed and spread through many cities in the GDR. Because of state pressure and control over freedom of assembly and expression, peace groups cannot organize, engage in direct confrontation with the state or stage mass protest marches, as do their West European counterparts. Thus, they have been forced to seek innovative ways of engaging in peace activity.

The first mass independent peace manifesto, the "Berlin

28

Appeal" (see Appendix II), was released on January 25, 1982, and eventually attracted more than 2,000 signatures. Drafted by the late Robert Havemann and East Berlin Pastor Rainer Eppelmann, it is believed to be the independent East German activists' response to the Krefeld Appeal, a single-issue petition to cancel the NATO decision to install Cruise and Pershing II missiles in West Germany, for which three million signatures were gathered. The Berlin Appeal deals with deeper, long-term problems of peace and human rights, although it also calls for the removal of all nuclear weapons from Europe. It raises the question of a divided Germany and calls for the withdrawal of the former Allies' (i.e., Soviet, American, British and French) occupation troops. The Berlin Appeal was the first independent peace manifesto in the 1980s to popularize the organic connection between freedom of expression and calls for removal of weapons and peace activity. Like the appeals that appeared after it in other East European nations and in the Soviet Union, the Berlin Appeal raised questions about war toys, peace studies, alternative service for conscientious objectors, civil defense, military parades, and conversion of military production towards aiding the Third World.[1]

The first major event of the peace movement to receive Western media attention was the Dresden "Peace Forum" in February 1982, a commemoration of the 37th anniversary of the destruction of Dresden. A demonstration was organized outside the Church of Our Lady in Dresden but the church authorities, alarmed at the potential for conflict with the state, transformed the demonstration into a peaceful discussion forum. This involved some 5,000 young people and a group of senior church representatives.

One issue discussed at the forum was the government's harassment of those who wore the peace movement's symbol, the "Swords into Ploughshares" badge. The symbol is a reproduction of a Soviet sculpture which stands outside the United Nations building in New York. The symbol's popularity worried the state, and it began to ban the badge in some schools, on occasion threatening those who wore it with expulsion from colleges and apprenticeships. Sometimes police went so far as to rip the badges off young people's clothing. The church at first supported demonstrators, but later, fearing state criticism, advised against the use of the symbol. Finally, the state adopted new laws which prohibited the use at meetings of signs or symbols which "abuse the interests of society." Such symbols, identified with independent sentiment, even when used in official settings were liable to threaten state control.

In the fall of 1983, hundreds of thousands of people took part in mass religious meetings in celebration of the 500th anniversary of the birth of Martin Luther, leader of the Protestant Reformation, who was born in Eisleben, in what is now East Germany. Luther, although a religious figure, was incorporated into the pantheon of heroes of socialism for the occasion. At that time, several hundred peace activists and Western friends planned to petition both the U.S. and Soviet embassies, calling for no new deployment of nuclear weapons. Despite preventive arrests of East Berliners and the expulsion of two West Germans, about 30 East Germans, joined by members of the West German Green Party and the Dutch peace movement, managed to demonstrate for an hour in an East Berlin square before they were arrested.

A series of other events took place in 1983, with activists

from Weimar distributing leaflets and spraying slogans on walls; groups in Potsdam demonstrating in the Square of Nations; peaceful protests in Leipzig; and demonstrations by women in East Berlin.

After NATO began to deploy intermediate-range missiles in Europe in the last months of 1983, followed by Soviet deployments in the GDR and Czechoslovakia, a large number of peace activists were either arrested, expelled or forced to emigrate from the GDR. There was concern among Western supporters that the GDR authorities no longer cared about the Western peace movement's protests of such treatment because the movement had lost much of its leverage when it lost the missile deployment battle.

In the summer of 1983, in a move that virtually destroyed the thriving peace community in Jena, East German authorities expelled 20 young peace activists to West Germany. Included in this group was Roland Jahn, who was handcuffed and forcibly put on a train to the West. Previously he had been given a suspended sentence for "slandering the state" when he rode through town on a bicycle carrying a Solidarity banner. Apparently one of the reasons that the Jena group became vulnerable to the crackdown was that it disassociated itself from the church.

In mid-December 1983, graphic artist Barbel Bohley and historian Ulrike Poppe, members of Women for Peace, were arrested and charged under Article 99 of the GDR Penal Code, which provides for up to eight years of imprisonment for "treasonable passing on of information" if that information is considered "to the disadvantage of the interests" of the GDR, and is passed on to "foreign organizations...and their helpers."[2] The

31

charges, later dropped, were based on a meeting with a British woman peace activist.

Women for Peace, which had a circle with over 100 participants at various times and gathered more than 500 names in its appeal to stop drafting women, had been active in independent peace conventions in East Berlin. On January 24, 1984, after 22 days of a hunger-strike, and numerous appeals from alarmed peace activists in many Western countries, Bohley and Poppe were released. Because the women were popular and known abroad, the authorities were forced to back down. It proved the continuing efficacy of Western protest. But even Western peace movement concern could not help everyone in trouble, especially if they were less well known. Sylvia Goethe, for example, a member of an unofficial peace group, was sentenced on April 20, 1984, to 20 months of imprisonment for having circulated information abroad "harmful to the GDR."

In recent years, the East German groups have tended to engage in quieter activities within the churches to avoid the discouraging attrition by arrests. East German authorities have moved to cut off the life-line with the Western peace movement by denying visas into East Berlin for more than 100 activists in West Germany. Other foreign peace activists have been expelled on occasion for contacting their colleagues. In October 1984, for example, members of a Danish peace group were deported after distributing leaflets and performing a play about disarmament. But, despite restriction on such contact, the GDR activists have managed to keep in touch with colleagues in the East as well as in the West. Western peace movement members continue to visit the activists who remain in the GDR, mainly in East Berlin; expulsions of peace group members are rare, but emigration is

32

increasingly common (see below).

Despite the hardening of official attitudes towards their work, independent activists nevertheless survived and even expanded cooperation with neighboring peace groups. In 1984, a joint statement was issued by independent peace activists in the GDR and Czechoslovakia, protesting the stationing of both Soviet and NATO missiles. A women's peace petition was launched among a number of East and West European countries and there were other appeals and cross-border meetings. The most recent and notable of the joint statements was issued in November 1986 entitled, "Giving Real Life to the Helsinki Accords," signed by individuals and groups in some 20 countries East and West, including East German peace and human rights activists (see Appendix VI).

The East German government was clearly embarrassed by the existence of an independent peace movement that linked socialists and Christians. Peace and disarmament issues had always been officially promoted and monopolized by the state policy and propaganda apparatus. The Church could join the chorus in a muted variation of the one-sided attacks on Western armaments, but never in direct opposition to Soviet bloc policies. When such criticism emerged, it could only be explained away by traditional dogma. The state claimed that peace activists are subversive, and dependent upon Western intelligence services. Officials such as Dieter Weiger of the Institute for International Affairs in East Germany said that pacifists are "against our security system, against our people's army."

John Sandford, a member of END and one of the best known chroniclers of GDR peace activism, summarized the state's posture vis-a-vis an authentic domestic peace movement

33

when he wrote about the reaction to the Berlin Appeal:

> The state -- alarmed at the prospect of an
> oppositional Marxist-Protestant alliance -- was clearly
> jittery, caught between an instinctive fear of
> subversion and the desire not to tarnish its image
> abroad.[3]

Eventually, the GDR peace activists, who had emerged from a background that lacked a tradition of widespread civil rights activism, found themselves more overtly involved in a struggle to gain civil liberties. In 1985, a new civil rights initiative grew out of the independent peace movement, launched by many of those who were leading peace spokespersons, such as Rainer Eppelman, Ralf Hirsch, and Wolfgang Templin. Their first appeal, in January 1985, was addressed to GDR leader Erich Honecker on the occasion of the United Nations Youth Year and called for full implementation of the U.N. Universal Declaration of Human Rights, particularly the rights to travel, speak, and assemble freely. More than three hundred people signed the petition, and they continued to draft a series of other rights appeals. In July 1985, an appeal was sent to the official youth organization, Free German Youth (FDJ), addressed to the participants of the International Youth Festival in Moscow. The signers stated plainly that they did not feel themselves represented by the FDJ and called for implementations of human rights, in particular, freedom of assembly and an end to travel restrictions to foreign countries -- including other countries in the Soviet bloc:

> ...it is not acceptable that citizens of the GDR are

34

turned back without explanation at the Czech border, that private trips to Poland are only possible in exceptional cases, that it is necessary to submit an application for travel to Hungary, Romania, Bulgaria and the Soviet Union, which can be refused without explanation. It is impossible for a GDR citizen to travel spontaneously to Moscow in order to experience the events of the World Festivals....Peaceful assembly and the founding of initiatives, organizations, associations, clubs and political parties should not be dependent on official permission. The unrestricted work of independent groups would protect the society from petrification in an inflexible administrative order that inhibits creativity among its citizens.[4]

In May 1985, the group sent a letter to Honecker protesting the prohibition of certain people entering the GDR (e.g., their friends in the West German peace movement), and in September 1985, the group issued an even bolder "Open Letter to the Government of the GDR" protesting the restriction of travel.

It is unacceptable that we should receive our rights only as a favor granted to us, provided that we refrain from independent political activity. We demand the repeal of the prohibition against foreign travel that has been imposed on us. Only the implementation of equal rights for all and a comprehensive expansion of freedom of travel will help persuade people to remain willingly in this country, thereby reducing the number of emigres.[5]

The appeals were signed by three spokespersons who gave their names and addresses, an approach used by Charter 77 in Czechoslovakia to signify the open, non-clandestine nature of their movement.

In June 1986, a samizdat publication entitled Grenzfall appeared for the first time in the GDR, produced by the membership of the Peace and Human Rights Initiative. At this writing, seven issues have appeared, with the eighth due in autumn 1987. Modest in its number of hectographed copies and its targeted readership, it is intended to be a monthly bulletin on peace, ecology and human rights issues, in addition to police repression and the development of independent initiatives in the GDR. The title literally means "borderline" in a legal sense, but it also conveys a number of meanings: composed of two words meaning "border" and "case" or "fall," it could refer to the borderline zone in which the opposition functions; or to that border which it is illegal to cross; or to the limits of freedom that are imposed by the state; or simply to the tumbling down -- the fall -- of the Wall itself. The appearance of Grenzfall, which is independent of both the state and the church, is a highly significant development in the growth of independent peace and human rights activity in East Germany.

Agitation for peace, for the improvement of the environment, and for the right to travel are by no means confined to East Berlin. Reports indicate that there is a group of 40 in Mecklenburg who meet regularly, and of meetings of 8 or more in Weimar. All in all it is claimed that there are groups in over 100 cities who maintain links with each other through their representatives, meeting at the various workshops and

Friedensdekaden -- "ten days of peace" -- seminars that are held within the church.

In the last several years, the government has changed its tactics in dealing with peace activists; instead of arresting them, the authorities are relying on financial and personal harassment. The names and addresses of the major spokespersons for peace and human rights are well known to the authorities. The periodic open letters, appeals or proposals sent to the government or to a Party Congress usually have up to 30 signatures and addresses. (There are also one-time mass petitions that attract thousands of names, but there have been fewer of these in recent years.) These initiatives are ignored by the government but they do get published in Western journals. There is ample ground for arrest under any one of a half dozen ambiguous statutes which severely punish "incitement hostile to the state," "treasonable passing of information," "public villification," "taking up illegal contacts," and so forth. The new policy of imposing fines and other means of aggressive harassment is similar to the tactics used against Charter 77 people in Czechoslovakia and Solidarity activists in Poland. Such activists lose their jobs; their children are harassed at school and deprived of higher educational opportunities; death threats come in the mail; telephone service becomes irregular and is frequently disconnected. When Gorbachev visited East Berlin this year, for example, state security police were posted outside the homes of activists for three days.

It seems clear that the state is not allowing itself to be provoked into creating any martyrs or <u>causes</u> <u>celebres</u> by imprisoning the activists. This is not a time for negative international publicity, especially with Gorbachev advocating

37

glasnost, and with improved relations with West Germany on the agenda.

But the financial oppression and harassment do take a heavy toll on personal lives and have been a factor in the emigration of activists to West Berlin. Whether they leave voluntarily or as an alternative posed by the government instead of arrest, the loss of people is a serious blow to the movement. Women for Peace, for example, has been decimated by emigration and has practically ceased to function.

In addition to attrition by emigration, the enormous task confronting the remaining activists is to make some headway among a passive and depoliticized population. East Germany is unique in the Eastern Bloc. It is a police state with an estimated 300,000 uniformed policemen and an unknown number of plainclothesmen that harshly represses all basic freedoms which has nevertheless achieved a certain kind of legitimacy in the eyes of its people. Unlike most of its East European neighbors, the GDR provides basic needs and economic security for its citizens at a level approximating some West European nations.

Conscientious Objection

Conscientious objection is not tolerated in East Germany. Socialism is for peace, but peace must be defended. When the Conscription Law was published in January 1962, the <u>Berliner Zeitung</u> stated:

> We support all young people in West Germany
> who refuse military service, for they are weakening

NATO's imperialist army. In the GDR there can and will be no refusal of military service, for we are protecting peace and Socialism.[6]

Anyone not wanting to serve under arms must join the army as a <u>Bausoldat</u>, construction soldier, which involves building airfields and other military facilities. The construction soldiers wear a spade emblem on their uniforms and are thus identifiable by the public and sometimes subject to scorn. But being recognizable to one another helps to strengthen ties in the autonomous peace movement. An estimated 500 young men a year choose this option. However, former construction soldiers face discrimination in employment based on their conscientious objector status. The <u>Totalverweigerer</u>, those who refuse both military and construction service, are sentenced to from 18-26 months in prison; there are an estimated 200 per year, about half of whom are Jehovah's Witnesses. Sometimes, COs are simply pronounced "unfit for service."[7] The following are examples of those sentenced to prison for conscientious objection.

o Michael Lieholt was sentenced to 9 months in prison beginning November 29, 1984, for refusing military service.
o Ralf Schirner was sentenced, also on November 29, 1984, to 20 months of imprisonment for conscientious objection.
o Approximately 40 conscientious objectors were imprisoned in September 1985. They were released a month later. The majority were "total objectors," refusing the option of unarmed construction. Others were

reservists who had done normal service but now wished to register as COs and were not allowed to do so. The release was apparently due to church pressure, and was also a good-will gesture following the German summit and in advance of a visit planned by Honecker to West Germany which subsequently did not take place. Some observers believe that the releases were used as a means of inducing the church to cancel a human rights seminar.

The Role of the Church

The independent peace movement is somewhat nurtured and protected from official persecution by the church, which provides an environment and facilities where young people can hold free discussions and peace activities. These kinds of activities within the church have been more or less tolerated, whereas street actions are strongly discouraged; about 500 peace activists have been sentenced in the last few years for leafletting, holding silent vigils or other peaceful demonstrations, or spray-painting anti-nuclear slogans on walls. But despite these arrests, low-key events continue to attract hundreds of people throughout East Germany. With the rapid spread of interest in peace among young people, the church has become increasingly outspoken on foreign policy issues, peace, the environment and domestic issues such as militarization, alcoholism and crime. The regime has cautiously allowed these issues to be discussed within the churches but has exacted loyalty to the main government programs in exchange, and has often coopted church leaders into one-sided attacks on Western armaments.

Since the church is the only institution in society in which

40

people can assemble freely, discuss social questions and publish material, its cooperation is important for the growth of any protest movement. However, the limits on how far the church can go on issues of civil and political rights versus questions of peace and ecology have led to increased tensions between human rights activists and even the more progressive pastors of the church. To understand the role of the church it is necessary to describe the special relation between the church and the state.

In a population of 17 million people there are about 7 million parishioners of the Evangelical Church. For many years after the Communist Party gained control of the state, it tried to implement its ideology of atheism by severely restricting the scope of church activities. In 1976, Pastor Brusewitz immolated himself in protest against the treatment of the church and he was soon followed by another pastor, Rolf Gunther.

On March 6, 1978, a deal was struck between Honecker, chairman of the Party, and Bishop Albrecht Schonheer. The church would be allowed to put up new buildings, have access to TV, import church literature from the West, run its own kindergartens, and visit prisons and old age homes after visiting hours. Clergy and church workers would be entitled to state pensions and the church would receive rent from the state for the use of its land (the church is a considerable landowner, possessing 500,000 acres) as well as government money for maintenance. There are six theological faculties at universities paid for entirely by the state. In exchange, the church became a "Kirche in Sozialismus", a church in socialism, a partner in the enterprise of maintaining a stable society.

A Helsinki Watch consultant who recently travelled to East Germany held meetings with a pastor who is active in the peace movement and a theologian who is prominent in world wide disarmament campaigns. The consultant's report on these meetings gives on indication of the church's attitude toward civil and political rights:

> While the church opposed aspects of the militarization of society and campaigned for better treatment of conscientious objectors, it was not in any sense a political critic of the state. The church considered that the issues of freedom of speech, press and assembly were used as fuel for Western propaganda against their "socialist system." The pastor agreed that the absence of these freedoms was a "defect" in their society that should be remedied at some point, but he was quick to counter that the homelessness, unemployment, insecurity and neglect of the elderly in the West were greater violations of human rights. The pastor asked what good it did a young man in West Berlin who had the right to travel if he could not afford to buy a ticket. When it was pointed out that huge numbers of people in the West do exercise their right to travel and that in any case the poverty of the youth in the West did not justify the denial of freedom to a wage-earning youth in the East, he smiled and admitted to being inconsistent. His agreeable concession revealed an awareness of his defensiveness on issues of civil and political rights. Fundamental loyalty to his society showed itself in a flash of emotion when the pastor spoke of those peace activists who had emigrated as having betrayed their country. He showed no awareness that the country

42

they were supposed to have betrayed had made it unbearable for many of them to stay. He also spoke with some contempt of people who he claimed became peace activists in order to be allowed to leave the country.

A continuing concern of his and many like him was how the West would misuse church criticism of the state for its cold-war aims. In illustration he told of a full day of festivities at his parish which included dancing, singing and childrens' games, all of which was shot by West German television crews. What appeared the next day on West German TV, which is seen by almost all East Germans, was less than one minute of the entire day -- showing the pastor praying for imprisoned conscientious objectors. This kind of coverage, he complained, distorted the role of the church.

He spoke of the radicalization of the peace activists which was creating problems for his continued cooperation. As an example, he referred to a poster which the activists had mounted in the church caricaturing a German general and which they had refused to remove; a year earlier, he said, they would have taken it down. Aside from its political implications, his problem with the poster was the possibility that a West German TV photographer might take its picture, beam it into East Germany and give the impression of an increasingly politicized parish. This would not sit well with either his parishioners or with his higher-ups.[8]

It is clear that if the church is beginning to feel uncomfortable with what it considers to be the politicization of the peace movement, then conflicts between the peace and human rights activists and the church are inevitable. A watershed event occurred in November 1986 with a seminar on "Human rights - the Individual and Society," one of the first seminars organized by East Germans and devoted entirely to human rights in the GDR. The seminar was supposed to have been held in January 1986 but was abruptly cancelled by the leadership of the Protestant church. It was finally allowed to take place on November 22 and 23, 1986, in the Friedichsfelde/Berlin parish of East Berlin. The original cancellation had moved the human rights petitioners to organize themselves into an initiative called Peace and Human Rights GDR. Only a few members of this group were invited to the seminar, which was contrary to the previous practice of allowing interested and active people working outside church circles to participate.

According to the Peace and Human Rights' summary of the seminar, the following problems were evident: the number of invitees was determined by the state; self-censorship was exercised; discussions were held strictly to a narrow agenda; a parish official acted as an observer at each of the six workshops; participants could not circulate petitions, inquiries, resolutions or collect signatures; and there was inadequate discussion of civil and political human rights. Thus, it became apparent during the November seminar that a truly independent forum for discussion would have to take place outside the church.

Another event connected with the "Kirchentag" ("Church

44

Day") which took place on June 24-27, 1987, revealed the
tensions within the church itself between Protestant youths and
their sympathetic pastors and high church officials. A Kirchentag
is an official gathering of Protestant officials, ministers and
laypeople for celebration and discussion of various church
matters but not excluding larger questions such as peace and
environmental issues. As this was to be the first gathering of
only East German Protestants (i.e. excluding West Germans) in
East Berlin since 1961 with the building of the Berlin Wall, the
Kirchentag had taken on special significance.

A church official, Gunter Krusche, announced in December
1986 that a Freidenswerkstatt ("Peace Workshop") -- a different
event sponsored by the church -- would not take place in 1987.
Many observers believe that this cancellation was designed by the
church to avoid any friction with the state so that the state
would not interfere with the Kirchentag. These peace
workshops, which have been held annually for the past 6-7
years, are meant to give youth groups inside the church the
opportunity to exchange views on peace issues and, to some
extent, on human rights. They had been quite spontaneous events
with relatively uncensored discussion, in addition to being
occasions for getting signatures for appeals and protest petitions.
Non-Protestant members of independent groups had been able to
participate. The cancellation of the workshop led to vigorous
protest by the pastors of the parishes where the workshops were
to have taken place. In response to the protests, the church
reconsidered and announced in January 1987 that the workshop
would be held in the fall, long after the Kirchentag had had its
undisturbed day.

Out of the conflict over the initial cancellation was born the

"Kirchentag von Unten," ("Kirchentag from Below"). The Kirchentag from Below is a loose coalition of mainly young people, both within the church and independent of it, who were dissatisfied with the policies of the church with regard to the Kirchentag. The Kirchentag from Below also disagreed with the church's relations with the "independents" (those outside the church) and on such issues as: ecology, peace, the third world, the church's role in social issues and what they saw as accomodations made with the state.[9] There were suggestions that during the Kirchentag, they would occupy a church and stage a sit-in to hold their own workshop. Even sympathetic pastors who had protested the cancellation were disturbed by this "radical" plan. The protesters had rejected the church's offer of a specific church in which they could gather on the grounds that its 2,000 seating capacity would not be adequate for the sit-in they expected.

On June 24, as reported by the Frankfurter Allgemeine Zeitung and reports on the Austrian Radio, between 1,200 and 2,000 protesters gave out leaflets at the opening service of the Kirchentag containing slogans like "If the church keeps being conformist, nothing will change." The sit-in did not take place. Instead they asked the sympathetic Bishop Forck of East Berlin to provide meeting space and were given rooms in two parish churches in East Berlin. On Saturday, June 27, about 600 protesters met with church leaders in one of those parishes to voice their criticism of the church for compromising with the state on "fundamental questions" and for not recognizing the work of the protestant youth as "a natural component" of the church's work. The "fundamental questions" ranged from issues of peace, environment, human rights, democracy, women's issues

46

and militarism to the discriminatory treatment of Christians, punks, gays and lesbians.

The size and vigor of the protest surprised the church leaders who had expected a few hundred fringe types like "punks and rockers." The protests were not only tolerated but genuine dialogue developed; church leaders spoke of the need to build a constructive relationship with the youth groups.

Although the state did not interfere with the Kirchentag, it had put pressure on the church to conduct most of the meetings behind closed doors, open only to those who had signed up for the particular session. The state was also not going to allow the church to use public facilities for any meetings, but it relented after much negotiation. Honecker himself decided to allow the use of a stadium for the concluding church service, a stadium which was quite far from downtown East Berlin. At this concluding church service, the protesting youths held up a banner calling for "Glasnost in the Church; Glasnost in the State," as well as other banners demanding the right to conscientious objection and funding for social projects.

In East Germany, it is within the church that the greatest possibilities for mobilizing against militarism and for human rights exist. Though the peace and human rights activists are cautiously striking out on their own, they still retain close connections with church peace activists. The Kirchentag from Below, both in its protest and in the symbolism of its name, reveals the discontent and impatience of the Protestant youth.

East Germany -- Notes

[1] John Sandford, <u>The Sword and the Ploughshare: Autonomous Peace Initiatives in East Germany</u>, END Special Report. London: Merlin Press, 1983, p. 58-67.

[2] <u>Amnesty International Report 1984</u>, Amnesty International Publications, London, 1984.

[3] Sandford, <u>op. cit.</u>

[4] "To the Participants in the XII World Festival of Youth and Students in Moscow," <u>Across Frontiers</u>, Winter 1985, Vol. 2, No.2.

[5] <u>Across Frontiers</u>, <u>op. cit.</u>, Vol. 2, No. 3-4.

[6] Sanford, <u>op. cit.</u>, p. 41.

[7] Ibid, p. 30.

[8] Stanley Engelstein, Trip Report, July 1987.

[9] Information supplied by Franek Michalski, August 1987.

III. HUNGARY

The prospect of war and the absence of democracy are two sides of the same reality: politicians threatening defenseless people.
George Konrad, Antipolitics.

Hungary's popular uprising was brutally crushed by Soviet tanks in 1956. Today, the presence of 65,000 Soviet troops keeps the memories alive. Citizens are not permitted to discuss the revolution publicly, although several unofficial events were organized in October 1986 on the 30th anniversary of the revolution.

Hungary is considerably less repressive than its Soviet bloc neighbors, particularly in the area of free expression. The authorities tend to rely on fines and harassment -- rather than imprisonment -- for those engaged in independent activity. Most of this activity centers around Hungary's vigorous samizdat (underground) press. A small "democratic opposition," made up largely of intellectuals, is more or less tolerated and a number of its leaders have been allowed to travel abroad for lecture and study. Nevertheless, independent initiatives -- including peace and environmental movements -- face obstruction and harassment by the state authorities.

Peace Issues

The Peace Group for Dialogue (Dialogus) -- to date, the only independent peace movement to have been formed in Hungary -- was organized in September 1982, primarily by

49

university students and recent graduates. During the brief span of its independent activity, the group attracted thousands of young people and organized a number of successful activities of the sort not normally tolerated in Eastern Europe. These included an officially sponsored peace march, several public meetings and a lecture by E.P. Thompson, leader of the British END (European Nuclear Disarmament).

After visiting the Dialogue members in Budapest in September 1982, E.P. Thompson wrote in Double Exposure that the group was closely informed about the Western peace movement, with whom they hoped to enter into direct relations, and that "the mood was that of a search for a third way among the younger European generations."[1] However, the group's efforts to operate openly and promote dialogue with the government led to increased efforts by the Hungarian authorities to coopt the movement.

In an article about Dialogue's approach, Miklos Haraszti, a writer and member of the democratic opposition, said that the Dialogue had reason to believe that the authorities might accept a compromise: the National Peace Council would tolerate the existence of an independent peace movement which would be an indication of political liberalization. In return, the Dialogue would agree to distance itself from the political opposition. Haraszti wrote:

> There is nothing new in the idea of such a compromise. In another form it was the strategy of the Kadar-era intelligentsia. But in order to gain official recognition, the earlier activists had been forced to choose between official control and

independence outside the law. The new peace movement assumed -- and proved to its own satisfaction -- that a realistic compromise was possible in its case, despite the discouraging precedents.[2]

As it turned out, Dialogue's willingness -- indeed, it's outright efforts -- to separate the peace issue from that of human rights and political opposition played directly into the hands of the authorities. Sacrificing the human rights component that threatened the authorities, as represented by the democratic opposition, made the group more vulnerable to government control. A number of statements made by Ferenc Koszegi, a Dialogue leader, were so hostile toward the "dissident" community that they echoed the government's attitude toward opposition activists. Referring to the dissidents as a "manipulating force," Koszegi wrote:

> The attempts of the opposition elements to gain prominent places in the emerging movement could be of great danger to the movement itself....The new movement has developed into a force which cannot be identified with either the Peace Council or with political opposition. It is and must remain an open and public movement, resisting all attempts at cooption and manipulation."[3]

The official Hungarian Peace Council (NPC) made numerous attempts to coopt the unofficial peace group. An official March 1983 report of the Central Committee Section for Party and Mass Organizations discussed the NPC's efforts in this regard, and indicating that the semi-legal activities of the Dialogue would not be tolerated much longer by the government and that peace movements outside the Peace Council would not be legalized. The report stated:

> The [Dialogue] group does not have any significant mass support, but its influence is growing. At the present moment, Dialogus groups are operating in Budapest, Szeged, Debrecen and Pecs. Their ideas are in equal measure mixed, immature and self-contradictory, even giving rise to controversy within their own circles...Pacifist efforts making their appearance in church and religious circles are also on the increase.
>
> The National Peace Council has taken up and continues to maintain contacts with the majority of spontaneous groups, and tries to influence their activities. ...The Party organs and organizations have not everywhere paid sufficient attention to directing and supervising the peace movement. Uncertainty can be observed as to how the new peace phenomena, and in particular the independent initiatives of the youth, are to be judged. The National Peace Council and the social organizations and movements have not been able to integrate the spontaneous peace initiatives within the bounds of their own framework.[4]

The Political Committee resolved that peace groups would be "brought into connection with the united movement directed by the National Peace Council," and that the Party should isolate and expose "those efforts which seek to use the peace movement as a pretext for questioning the peace policies of our Party and government, our commitments to our allies, and the initiatives for peace of the Soviet Union and the socialist community."[5]

In May 1983, the authorities reversed their prior decision and refused to grant passports to Dialogue members who were planning to attend an international peace conference in West Berlin. In July 1983, officials prevented the group from holding an international peace camp in Hungary by refusing visas, expelling Western pacifists, and detaining about 20 Dialogue activists. Soon afterward, the group disbanded, saying that its chief aim -- dialogue with the authorities -- had become effectively impossible. The experience of Dialogue made clear that the Hungarian authorities were unwilling to permit an independent peace movement operating outside the confines of the National Peace Council.

Although Dialogue no longer exists, some of its members have pursued other forms of peace activity. One of the group's founders, Ferenc Koszegi, formed a network of "Peace Clubs" which met regularly but were virtually coopted by the National Peace Council; other Dialogue members continue to engage in small-scale independent activity. Rabbi Csenyi, who had served time in jail for advocating conscientious objection, was reported to have begun a new Jewish peace group in Budapest in early 1984.

During an official signature campaign against the NATO deployment of nuclear missiles in Western Europe in the fall of 1983, some high school students began circulating a counter-petition, protesting that the issue of Soviet deployment had not been addressed. Two school principals were reportedly fired for failing to stop the students' petitions.

Conscientious Objection

Hungarian law does not allow for conscientious objection. Article 336 of the Criminal Code provides for sentences of up to five years of imprisonment for those who refuse military service. Since 1977, however, members of some small, Christian groups, such as the Nazarenes and the Seventh Day Adventists, have been permitted to do unarmed military service. The Hungarian authorities have not extended this right to the Roman Catholics. Amnesty International's 1986 Report states that as many as 150 conscientious objectors were serving time in Baracska prison, most of whom were Jehovah's Witnesses who had refused to perform any kind of military service.[6] The government's position toward conscientious objection was articulated by Imre Miklos, the State Secretary for Religious Affairs, who stated that conscientious objectors are committing an "offense against their families and countrymen" and that their position is "morally untenable."

In an article printed in The New York Times on August 15, 1987, Miklos Haraszti called upon the Helsinki Review Conference in Vienna -- part of the ongoing CSCE (Conference on Security and Cooperation in Europe) process -- to address the right to conscientious objection and alternative service in Eastern Europe. He wrote:

> Warsaw Pact rigidity on the issue [of conscientious objection] has become increasingly untenable because of the growing number of objectors

54

and, more important, because the objectors have begun to demand their rights publicly. The longer the Warsaw Pact's new detente campaign goes on, the more difficult it will be for its members to justify their hard line toward antimilitarists. This is especially true in Poland and Hungary, whose governments want to maintain a liberal image.

The only armed conflicts in Europe in the last 40 years have occurred when the Soviet Union used Warsaw Pact armies to repress democratic ferment. Thus, objection to military service in the bloc is not only a matter of religious principle but also an indication of popular, nonviolent, democratic resistance and solidarity....The easy verifiability of such an agreement makes it eminently suitable for the Helsinki framework: either the objectors are in prison or their rights are being respected....If indeed the Helsinki spirit couples European security and the freedom of the individual, then the right of conscientious objection embodies this spirit.[7]

Government actions against conscientious objectors have included the following:

o   During the first week of September 1985, a military court in Budapest tried 11 cases of conscientious objectors and sentenced 10 Jehovah's Witnesses and one Roman Catholic to prison terms ranging from two years and six months to two years and ten months.

o   On August 28, 1985, the police arrested Gyorgy

55

Hegyi, 19 years old. After the arrest, his home was searched and religious and underground publications were confiscated. Hegyi's parents were not allowed to enter the court during their son's trial, despite the fact that trials in military courts are usually open to the immediate relatives of the defendant. Hegyi was sentenced to two years and ten months of imprisonment, but must serve his sentence in a penitentiary. (This is a medium degree of severity and permits the prisoner fewer privileges than in a less severe prison category.)

The reason that Hegyi was sentenced to a more severe prison category seems to involve his Catholic faith. Since the Catholic Church does not specifically forbid military service, the court concluded that Hegyi was merely following his own convictions. "There are aggressive crimes and there are crimes committed from fanaticism," the state attorney said. "However, the most dangerous crimes are committed from conviction based on philosophy." Hegyi's philosophy on military service is explained in a letter he sent to the draft board, in which he offered to serve a period of peaceful service with the army even longer than the normal period, provided he would not be required to carry arms.

On February 25, 1987, Zsolt Keszthelyi -- the first political, as opposed to religious, conscientious objector in Hungary -- was arrested under Article 336. He was sentenced to three years of imprisonment on April 27, reduced on appeal to 2-1/2 years on May 28. Keszthelyi, 23 years old and a dissident magazine editor, sent his draft papers back to the recruitment center on

56

February 18 with a statement explaining his refusal to serve in the Hungarian military:

> I, the undersigned Zsolt Keszthelyi, hereby declare that I wish to refuse military service because of political motives. I am not inclined to put my trust in a "people's democratic" army which is not placed under the control of a government elected by universal suffrage involving competing political programs. I think that by this action, just like by my struggle for a free press, I can contribute to the creation of a society which is free of fear and in which the management of social affairs is determined by the responsibility and conscience of individuals and not by unquestioning faith and fear. If there is no other way, I am ready to throw in my lot with those conscientious objectors who, due to their decision of conscience, have been sentenced to prison during the "people's democratic" periods of the past 40 years having penalties designed to deny true constitutionalism.[8]

Keszthelyi also addressed a letter about his case to the Helsinki Review Conference in Vienna.

Keszthelyi belonged to an independent youth group, Vox Humana, and has been an editor of the samizdat journal Egtajak Kozott (Between the Points of the Compass). Prior to Keszthelyi's recruitment, the authorities had undertaken several actions against him and the organizations with which he was affiliated: on January 30, 1987, the Hungarian official weekly

Elet es Irodalom (Life and Literature) published a strong attack against Egtajak Kozott; on February 4, police raided his apartment (in addition to the apartment of another editor of Egtajak Kozott, Jozsef Talata) and confiscated numerous samizdat publications, including 350 copies of a new samizdat journal. It seems likely that Keszthelyi was drafted as a means of punishing him for his independent activities.[9]

On March 29, 1987, the independent peace movement in Poland, Freedom and Peace, sent a cable to the Hungarian Embassy in Warsaw demanding the release of Keszthelyi.[10] In addition, a "Zsolt Keszthelyi Committee" was formed in Budapest on April 27.[11] At this writing, Keszthelyi remains in prison.

Some members of Catholic basis communities, associated with dissident Piarist priest Gyorgy Bulanyi, a widely known pacifist, have encouraged conscientious objection to military service. The Bulanyists challenge both the Hungarian authorities and the Catholic church hierarchy, which has a history of supporting the establishment. The basis communities have rejected the leadership of the church hierarchy based on what they consider to be compromises made with a totalitarian state; they challenge the government on moral and social issues, particularly with regard to obligatory military service. According to Keston College, over 20 members of Bulanyi's basis communities have been imprisoned for conscientious objection since 1979.[12]

o   In 1982, Cardinal Laszlo Lekai denied Father Bulanyi the right to celebrate Mass on the grounds that his theological teachings contradicted Roman Catholic doctrine. At least eight other Roman Catholic priests who

58

are allied with Father Bulanyi have been removed from their parishes.

o   Two Roman Catholic conscientious objectors who belonged to basis communities were adopted as Prisoners of Conscience by Amnesty International in 1984 -- Laszlo Habos, from Erd, and Jozsef Ujvari, from Tok. They were both convicted under Article 336 and were sentenced to 30-and 33-month prison terms, respectively, for refusing military service on grounds of conscience.

In a letter to the Budapest Cultural Forum, a Helsinki review meeting held in October 1985, Karoly Kiszely, a Hungarian activist who has spoken out on behalf of Catholic conscientious objectors, stated that there were a total of 150 Hungarians imprisoned for conscientious objection, either for refusing service without arms or for refusing the draft entirely. The letter urged the representatives of Helsinki signatory nations to consider their plight. Earlier in 1985, Hirmondo published an open letter by Kiszely to Cardinal Laszlo Lekai urging him "in the name of basic humanity and decency" to do everything possible to resolve the situation of Catholic conscientious objectors "who have been imprisoned and vilified on the basis of your false information." [13]

Environmental Issues

In the past few years, the ecologist or "green" movement has become the largest independent movement in Hungary. The movement is largely concerned with protesting the construction

of the Gabcikovo-Nagymaros Dam on the Hungarian Danube --
a joint project of the Czechoslovak and Hungarian governments,
to be financed also by the Austrian government -- but other
environmental concerns have also been addressed. In 1987,
however, the environmental movement has been less active than
it was in 1984-86. This is due largely to the fact that the
Hungarian government has decided to go forward with the
project; accordingly, the battle over the dam is subsiding.

Several independent, environmental organizations have been
formed in Hungary, starting with the Association for the
Protection of the Danube Region in 1983, followed by the Duna
Kor (Danube Circle) in 1984, the Blues and the Friends of the
Danube in 1985, and, most recently, the Danube Association in
1987. In addition, numerous independent actions have been
undertaken, including circulating petitions, holding meetings,
leafletting and other means of creating public awareness about
the environment.[14]

As was the case with the Dialogue group, the environmental
movement in Hungary often tried to distance itself from the
political opposition and conduct exclusively ecological actions --
specifically, to focus on the construction of the dam -- in order
to enhance its position with the government and to attract a
larger following. Included in this approach was an effort to gain
legal recognition by the government for the Association and
Duna Kor, a process that the authorities obstructed for months
and to which they never responded satisfactorily. The main goal
of the environmental movement -- to open up public debate on
the construction of the dam -- was proving to be as elusive as its
efforts to remain apolitical and nonconfrontational.

The government's persistent refusal to allow environmental

groups to operate in the official, legal fashion that they sought forced the groups into a more oppositional stance. In an article that appeared in a 1986 issue of Beszelo, Gyula Denes discussed the government's reaction to the movement: "The Hungarian political leaders reacted to the environment protection movement as they would have done to any autonomous movement; when they could not stop it, they branded it as a public enemy."[15] Though the authorities did not imprison the environmentalists, they did call in many of them for "warning talks" and orchestrated a press campaign against the movement.

One of the principal organizations fighting against the dam project has been Duna Kor, which was formed in the winter of 1984. In December 1985, Duna Kor was given an award by the London-based Friends of Right Livelihood Foundation. In an acceptance speech made by Janos Vargha, a biologist and leading environmentalist in Hungary, Vargha discussed the effects that the dam would have on the environment. He asserted that the project would:

> essentially change the hydraulic, physical, chemical and biological conditions of a nearly 200 kilometer section of the river itself and also that of the surrounding groundwater. These changes would be harmful to the drinking water supply, the quality of river and ground water, agriculture, forests and fish as well as the picturesque landscape.[16]

In order to distribute the prize money (once it finally made its way into Hungary) for environmental initiatives in Hungary, Duna Kor established the Danube Foundation in June 1987. The

61

Foundation, which is supposed to begin operating in September 1987, will be among the first independent foundations to distribute money for social purposes. However, since the foundation was formed without official permission, it remains to be seen how the authorities will react when the foundation begins operating.

Also established was the Danube Association, which was to be a more activist group than the foundation, comprised of environmentalists and respected intellectuals. The Association held two unofficial meetings in spring 1987, attended by 100-150 people. In June 1987, the Association applied for permission to form an official organization and announced plans to hold its first official meeting. But the government never approved the application and the day before the meeting was to take place, the organizers were informed that they were forbidden to hold such a meeting. Reports indicate that the Association published its correspondence with the authorities in a samizdat journal and protested the government's ban. At this writing, no further information is available.

Duna Kor itself has effectively ceased its activities.

The Hungarian authorities have not permitted any of the independent environmental groups to register as official organizations. In addition, their statements are ignored by the official press and their leaders are often harassed. Yet the environmental movement benefitted from the Hungarian government's own reluctance with regard to the dam project; the government has backed away from the project on two separate occasions since it was first planned in the early 1950s and has commissioned several economic and environmental studies of the project.[17] But despite the government's past uncertainty, the project is currently moving forward.

The Blues, formed in 1985, take their name as a kind of complement to the Greens but indicating that their primary concerns are water issues, notably protection of the Danube and drinking water supplies. The Blues do not have any formal membership or regular publications; they are young people who considered the coverage of the dam project in the official press as grossly inadequate. In order to disseminate their environmental information, the Blues began printing and distributing leaflets "to reach every corner of society." An interview with a member of the Blues printed in Hirmondo described their tactics as follows:

> Since the authorities had blocked all avenues of public debate, we have to choose a means of address that they can not control. This is the aspect we would like to maintain. However this does mean that we do not have direct personal contacts with people aware of environmental issues, so that it is not easy for anyone to join us. The Danube Circle has a different, legalistic approach, but this too has its drawbacks. They are in contact with experts and sympathizers, but since they act openly, the police can keep an eye on them. Although less able to engage in such organized activity, we can at least achieve our main aim all the more effectively; the wider dissemination of information. I don't believe that many people in the country are even aware that a power station is being planned on the Danube.[18]

In many respects, environmental issues -- specifically those relating to the Danube project -- have succeeded in galvanizing the Hungarian public more than any other issue. Some 10,000 people have signed protest statements and numerous others have attended meetings or been involved in the publication of underground pamphlets. As Judit Vasarhelyi, a leader of Duna Kor, told The Washington Post:

> The Danube movement is becoming a protest for democratization. It's being done by people who a few years ago wouldn't have thought of taking such a stance. And it's showing that civic courage is increasing.[19]

New environmental groups continue to emerge in Hungary, despite the relative inactivity of the environmental movement. In 1986, an environmental periodical called Vizjel (Water Mark) appeared, and in the past year, five issues have been produced. The journal deals with a range of environmental problems, from the dam project to dangerous waste dumps to studies of environmental movements in socialist countries. The authorities have harassed those involved in the publication, and have undertaken house searches to confiscate their materials. Moreover, the editor of Vizjel, Ferenc Langmar, was fired from his job in early 1987.[20]

The Hungarian government openly criticizes independent environment activity. An article that appeared in the official journal Magyar Hirlap on April 24, 1987, held that:

> there are in our society written and unwritten rules,

political and moral norms for the cooperation of organizations formed by the government power and society which include spontaneous, individual or group organizations. Could an action, for example, of a narrow group, accompanied by noisy foreign publicity, take root or lead to any "result" in our political structure, when this group -- holding itself aloof from dialogue -- opposes the governmental decision handed down in an interstate agreement, the building of the Bos-Nagymaros river barrage system, by stretching the truth and fanning national sentiments? Yet, this is the aim of several members of the small group calling itself by various names....they write petitions and spread pamphlets in which they stubbornly repeat already considered or even professionally unfeasible views. But when they call themselves representatives of Hungarian society, with the participation of protestors mainly imported from abroad, from Austria, and they organize a street demonstration...then there is hardly any more place for tolerance....[21]

The following are examples of the environmental actions that have been undertaken in Hungary:

o   In September 1985, the Blues distributed 10,000 leaflets around the country protesting the government's decision to build the dam. They also sent letters to members of parliament and intellectuals who lived in the Danube region explaining the economic and environmental problems that the dam would create.[22]

o   On February 7, 1986, Budapest police armed with truncheons attacked the participants in a peaceful demonstration that took place along the Danube. The demonstration was staged by some 20 Hungarian and 60 Austrian environmentalists to protest the construction of the dam. The demonstration was originally scheduled to include several hundred participants, but it was called off at the last minute because of a "lack of guarantees that the scheduled march would take place without violence." Janos Vargha, speaking for Duna Kor, said that they were warned not to proceed with the demonstration on the grounds that it would "violate the public good and endanger public safety." Those who participated in the march apparently had not learned of the cancellation, and when they arrived at the arranged meeting place, the area was full of police and secret police.[23]

The decision to cancel the demonstration sparked considerable controversy within the environmental movement. Duna Kor was criticized both for organizing the march and then for bowing to governmental pressure to cancel it.

o   In 1985 and 1986, 2,655 people signed a petition requesting a referendum on the dam project. In a letter to the petitioners, the government responded that there was no reason for a referendum since experts had already determined the merits of the project.[24]

o   In January 1986, environmentalists from Hungary, Austria and West Germany held an open meeting in a Budapest restaurant and signed a statement declaring that they would "use all democratic, peaceful and constitutional means" to change the Hungarian and Austrian governments' decision to build the Nagymaros dam. It was the first time that independent "Green" movements from East and West agreed to conduct a joint campaign in a Communist country.[25]

o   On April 16, 1986, a full-page advertisement appeared in the Austrian newspaper Die Presse, signed by Hungarian activists and intellectuals. The ad was in the form of an appeal addressed to the Austrian public to prevent the building of the Gabcikovo-Nagymaros Danube Power Plant, signed by a group of 30 Hungarian intellectuals. The appeal stated:

> We are approaching you this way because you could, in the near future, play a decisive role in financing and implementing a needless and harmful Czechoslovak-Hungarian Danube water power plant project.

> You ought to know that the Gabcikovo-Nagymaros project for a barrage dam system is facing peaceful but resolute and distinct resistance in Hungary. This has been the most significant manifestation of the citizens' will in the country for decades. Ten thousand opponents of the project have voiced their opinions in petitions, an open discussion and a referendum, but the government does not permit any media criticism nor does it allow any organization or rally to voice opposing views -- be it even by means of a "silent march."

The appeal goes on to give information about the

project, the discussion in Hungary and the consequences of Austrian participation. It was signed by leading opposition intellectuals including Sandor Csoori, Miklos Haraszti, Janos Kenedi, Janos Kis, Gyorgy Konrad, Laszlo Rajk, Janos Vargha.[26]

In the wake of the Chernobyl accident, Hungarian environmentalists were cautious about raising the nuclear power issue. On August 11, 1986, the Christian Science Monitor quoted one leader, Ivan Baba, as saying that "opposing nuclear power means opposing the Soviet Union, which helps us build nuclear plants. If we want to exist, we have to avoid criticism of such a sensitive subject." On August 14, Moscow's Izvestia announced that a new agreement on further joint development of nuclear power was signed between the Soviet Union and Hungary, which would begin with the installation of two reactors.

However, environmentalists have continued to be active and, since Chernobyl, their activities have included the following:

o   In late May 1987, a group of law students at the University of Budapest published an environmental bulletin. Reports indicate that the bulletin has been widely distributed.

o   In June 1987, environmentalists from the organization Global 2000 occupied the Austrian Embassy in Budapest. The nonviolent action was designed to protest Austria's participation in the construction of the Nagymaros dam, and the group called for an ecological commission to study the effect that the power plant would have on the environment.[27]

Thus far, the efforts of the environmental movement in Hungary have been unable to halt the construction of the Nagymaros dam, and the movement has been further weakened by its own internal divisions. Yet the movement continues. In an article that appeared in the August-September 1986 issue of Hirmondo (reprinted in Across Frontiers), a member of the Blues summed up the environmentalists' dilemma:

> It is extremely difficult to come up with new alternatives now that the public debates and presentations have come to a close, after the collection of signatures, efforts to form associations, after distributing leaflets, after the election battles. There have been advertisements in foreign papers, we tried to organize a protest walk but it was prevented, tried to initiate a referendum but it was rejected, and there is no room for us in the official press, so we write in samizdat publications. Our basic goals are the same. United together, it might be easier to find a way out.[28]

Despite recent setbacks, the environmental movement has played an important part in raising the consciousness of Hungarian society in terms of both civic courage and the environmental crisis.

Notes -- Hungary

[1] E.P. Thompson, Double Exposure. London: The Merlin Press, 1985.

[2] Miklos Haraszti, "Dialogue -- Hungary's Independent Peace Movement, Across Frontiers, Winter-Spring 1985.

[3] Ferenc Koszegi and E.P. Thompson, The New Hungarian Peace Movement. London: END-Merlin Press, 1983.

[4] Campaign for Peace & Democracy East/West, Peace & Democracy News, Winter 1984-5.

[5] Ibid.

[6] Amnesty International, Report 1986.

[7] Miklos Haraszti, "If Eastern Europeans Object to Military Service," The New York Times, August 15, 1987.

[8] Amnesty International Urgent Action, April 9, 1987.

[8] Hungarian October Information Service, London: February 23, 1987.

[10] Hungarian October Information Service, April 8, 1987.

[11] Hungarian October Information Service, April 27, 1987.

[12] John Eibner, "'The Hope of the Church': Basis Groups in Hungary," Frontier, Keston College, March-April 1987.

[13] Istvan B. Gereben, ed., Defiant Voices: Hungary 1956-1986. Center Square, PA: Alpha Publications, 1986.

[14] Gyula Denes, "The Politics of Environmental Protection," East European Reporter, Vol. 2, No. 2.

[15] Ibid.

[16] Text of Janos Vargha's acceptance speech provided by Friends of Right Livelihood Foundation, New York.

[17] Jackson Diehl, "Danube Plans Rile Hungarians," The Washington Post, December 15, 1985.

[18] East European Reporter, Vol. 2, No. 2.

[19] Diehl, op. cit.

[20] Across Frontiers, Vol. 3, No. 3, Summer-Fall 1987.

[21] Foreign Broadcast Information Service, June 5, 1986.

[22] "Danube Blues," East European Reporter, Vol. 2, No. 2.

[23] Foreign Broadcast Information Service, February 21, 1986.

[24] East European Reporter, Vol. 2, No. 2.

[25] Patrick Blum, "Greens Plan Budapest Protest," <u>Financial Times</u>, January 22, 1986.

[26] <u>Foreign Broadcast Information Service</u>, April 28, 1986.

[27] <u>Foreign Broadcast Information Service</u>, June 22, 1987.

[28] <u>Across Frontiers</u>, Summer-Fall 1987.

IV. POLAND

The struggle for peace is always a struggle for moral values, since the only authentic peace is one based on those values....Peace does not mean obedience to the more powerful; peace is not enslavement. Therefore, the struggle for peace is conceivable only as a struggle against totalitarian enslavement. -- Adam Michnik, Collection of Essays Published in German entitled <u>Polnischer Frieden</u>.

When the Polish authorities imposed martial law in December 1981, their aim was to reverse the process of democratization that had begun 16 months earlier with the creation of Solidarity. Although martial law was technically lifted in July 1983, many of its repressive features were incorporated into the Polish legal system. In addition, the government banned many independent organizations, including the Journalists Association, the Writers Union, the Independent Students Union and others.

Thousands of Polish activists have served time in prisons, jails and internment camps. At least 84 activists have died at the hands of the security forces. Yet despite the trauma that Polish society has suffered in the six years since the imposition of martial law, independent movements continue: Solidarity still claims several hundred thousand dues-paying members; thousands of individuals participate in an independent cultural life; and hundreds of books and periodicals are published underground each year.

Solidarity has never expressly included peace issues in its program, but several union activists, including some of its foremost thinkers, Jacek Kuron and Adam Michnik, have made a number of statements to the Western peace movement. When three Solidarity activists went on trial in 1985, Michnik, one of the defendants, urged members of the international peace movement to come to Gdansk and try to attend the trial, saying that "perhaps your presence might be decisive to our fate." Some Western activists responded to Michnik's appeal, including members of the Campaign for Peace & Democracy East/West.

The formation of an independent peace movement in Poland is a product of the Solidarity movement and its support as well as of contacts with the Western peace movement. This peace movement is known as Freedom and Peace, or WiP, by its Polish acronym. WiP was founded in April 1985, and soon established itself as a movement focusing on the militarization of Polish society and the right to alternative military service; struggling for international human rights; concerned with ecological issues; and committed to seeking nonviolent solutions to social problems.

WiP was initially formed by a group of young people to protest the imprisonment of Marek Adamkiewicz, who received a 2-1/2 year sentence for refusing to take a military oath pledging fraternal alliance with the Soviet Union. While other young men had refused to take the oath, Adamkiewicz was the first to be imprisoned for the offense, and he was treated as a common criminal. Friends of Adamkiewicz from several Polish cities, many of whom knew each other and Adamkiewicz from their involvement with the Independent Student Union (NZS), undertook a series of actions of his behalf. In March 1985, 12 people from Warsaw, Szczecin and Poznan staged a week-long hunger strike in Podkowa Lesna (near Warsaw) to demand Adamkiewicz's release. A seminar on peace and human rights was conducted during the strike, and more than 1,000 signatures

74

were collected on a petition to the authorities. It was during that seminar that the idea for establishing WiP was formed.

Since its inception, WiP has underscored the indivisibility of the struggles for peace and human rights. In a statement addressed to the END (European Nuclear Disarmament) Conference in Amsterdam in July 1985, WiP articulated its position:

> Peace to us is not only a matter of disarmament and international relations, it is also the individual attitudes of citizens and relations within a country.... As long as nations are oppressed, exploited, terrorized and slaughtered, there is no peace on earth, regardless of whether the oppressors are alien armies or native governments.... We propose...to permanently include the justice and freedom of citizens in the notion of peace; to treat the struggle against totalitarian systems as equal to the efforts toward disarmament...[1]

The idea that peace and human rights are integrally linked had been well articulated by Charter 77 in Czechoslovakia (see Chapter I, Czechoslovakia). In recent years, independent peace movements of the East and West have devoted much attention to this link. WiP, in addition to other independent groups in Eastern Europe, has consistently pushed for the inclusion of human rights in the peace discussion.

The nature of this dialogue can be seen in a November 1986 memorandum addressed to the CSCE Review Conference in Vienna entitled "Giving Real Life to the Helsinki Accords," (see Appendix VI) which was signed by groups and individuals in some 20 countries, East and West, including many WiP activists. The memorandum states: "A lasting detente cannot be bought at the cost of playing down the question of civil liberties and human -- political and social -- rights. Peace and security, detente and cooperation, basic rights and self-determination of peoples have to be achieved all together."[2]

In its Declaration of Principles (see Appendix III), issued on November 17, 1985, in Gdansk, Krakow, Warsaw and Wroclaw, WiP set forth its principal areas of concern.[3] The document lists seven issues to which WiP addresses itself: human rights; national liberation; the threat of war and the international peace movement; environmental protection; world hunger, humanitarian assistance; human development; and tolerance. It articulated its aims as follows:

> The "Freedom and Peace" movement takes as its first foundation the struggle for human rights, religious freedom and national independence.
>
> At the present time, the world faces the imminent threat of war, the consequences of which may be irreversible for human civilization. Many Poles are not aware of the reality of this threat, and treat it as an invention of Communist propaganda. Many Poles are not aware of the seriousness of the threat of nuclear war, of the problem of militarism and of a militaristic education. The second foundation of the "Freedom and Peace" movement is to change this situation. ...
>
> The "Freedom and Peace" movement takes non-violent resistance as its basic means of struggle against

76

evil. Non-violence provides the most difficult, yet the most appropriate means for social struggle for human rights. ...

As of this writing, WiP is a loose federation of groups in 11 Polish cities, the four main centers being Warsaw, Krakow, Gdansk and Wroclaw. (The other cities are Szczecin, Gorzow, Katowice, Bydgoszcz, Czestochawa, Kolobrzez and Poznan.) Of the 11 groups in Poland, six have their own bulletins. WiP is also translating and distributing Amnesty International's bulletins on human rights violations worldwide and has produced reports on such topics as WiP and the Greens; the Vienna Memorandum and the Prague Appeal; Otto Schimek (an Austrian soldier in World War II who was executed for refusing to shoot Polish civilians); individual peace treaties; and nuclear energy. There are roughly 100-200 WiP activists in Poland, but hundreds more supporters often participate in their actions. This is reflected by the fact that WiP has held demonstrations in which over 2,000 people participated and petition campaigns bearing some 10,000 signatures.

WiP avoids formal membership and hierarchy in its movement. It claims that its structure is built on friendships and, as such, is difficult to destroy. In order to be a member of WiP, one has to be willing to take part in its activities and, accordingly, risk reprisal from the authorities. WiP is aware that much of its potential constituency is afraid of independent initiatives and the fines, denials of passports and other reprisals such activities frequently incur.

WiP has undertaken numerous actions for peace, conscientious objection, ecology and human rights, and has involved a wide spectrum of young people with varying political and religious viewpoints. In the first three months of 1987, for example, WiP organized actions against torture in Afghanistan, the arrest of peace and human rights activists in Czechoslovakia, Hungary and Yugoslavia, and the construction of a nuclear plant in Zarnowiec.

The diversity of the movement makes it difficult to classify WiP's program. Concerns of WiP groups in various Polish cities reflect the range of tendencies that form the movement -- from vehement "anti-Soviet" positions, to largely ecological concerns, to pacifism, to anti-abortion and religious issues, to international human rights.

It is also important to note that WiP is an open movement. Those who sign WiP documents list their names and addresses and engage in civil disobedience which serves both to emphasize the moral character of their concerns and to irritate the Polish authorities. In a 1986 article by Franek Michalski, WiP leader Jacek Czaputowicz commented on WiP's above-ground activity: "Open action is also the safest action. We are doing nothing illegal, only demanding the right of every citizen to be free of political coercion in matters of personal/ethical decisions, such as military service."[4]

WiP has adopted Otto Schimek, an Austrian Wehrmacht soldier executed in 1944, as a kind of hero for its movement. WiP contends that Schimek was executed for refusing to follow orders to kill Polish civilians. There is considerable uncertainty surrounding the actual circumstances of his execution (which German records indicate was for "desertion and cowardice in the face of the enemy"),[5] and the Polish authorities have gone to some lengths in a campaign against the Schimek legend. For

WiP, however, the importance of Otto Schimek involves his refusal to follow orders blindly as required by a disciplined army. The fact that Schimek was a German soldier has added significance for WiP in its struggle against nationalism.[6]

In bi-annual pilgrimages to Schimek's grave in Machowa, WiP activists are consistently subjected to police harassment and fines. The only exception was on May 10, 1987, when a group of some 70 Western peace activists and WiP participants travelled to Machowa at the conclusion of WiP's seminar in Warsaw (see below). Police simply filmed the participants without making any attempts at further obstruction.

Peace Issues and Conscientious Objection

Although Solidarity has always been committed to non-violence as a tactic, its priority has remained trade union and civil rights activities. Solidarity has not been involved in general peace and disarmament issues and the right of conscientious objection. WiP is the only opposition group in Poland that has included a struggle against the nuclear threat among its goals, and has sought the right to conscientious objector status and the rejection of the oath under which military recruits in Poland must pledge fraternal alliance with the Soviet Union. As Piotr Niemczyk put it in an interview with the Hungarian samizdat journal Hirmondo:

> We are the children of Solidarity, our views have
> their roots in the Solidarity program. But Solidarity is
> a trade union and a trade union has tasks other than

concern for conscientious objection. Freedom and Peace is very close to Solidarity as far as its principles are concerned, but its sphere of activities differs.[7]

Refusal to take the military oath in Poland (under which recruits must pledge "to safeguard peace relentlessly in the fraternal alliance with the Soviet Army and other allied armies") is punishable by imprisonment, and several WiP members have been sentenced to prison terms on these grounds. Their imprisonment has elicited protests from international peace and human rights groups, in addition to protests in Poland. The Polish Helsinki Committee reported that on May 30, 1985, academic lawyers from Warsaw University stated that the present Polish law with regard to the military oath is "extremely unsatisfactory and requires changes... It is difficult for the theory of law to accept a situation in which certain recruits can be sent to prison for a long term for refusing to pronounce a few sentences."[8]

Two years of military service is compulsory in Poland and refusal to serve carries a penalty of five years of imprisonment, as stipulated under Article 231 of the Universal Defense Duty Act of November 21, 1967. Those who "persistently evade" military service face up to ten years of imprisonment. In addition to those with health problems, the following categories of people are excluded from the draft: the only family member earning an income; the only one able to operate a farm; coal miners; and those in religious seminaries.[9]

WiP contends that the right to alternative military service is in fact embodied in Articles 140 and 141 of the Universal Defense Duty Act. These articles state that alternative service can be performed in such areas as health service, environmental protection, social and public services. In an article by Piotr Niemczyk in the Warsaw WiP bulletin, a draftee should be able to qualify for alternative service on grounds that are "independent of the military; moral considerations, personal philosophy or religion." Nevertheless, the decision of whether alternative service is to be granted resides with the military and remains arbitrary, as the following cases illustrate:

o   The WiP information office reported 36 cases of conscientious objection between October 20, 1986, and April 12, 1987. Of these, 25 requested alternative service; the others involved a refusal to take the military oath or bear arms. WiP has reported that most applications for alternative service are not answered by the authorities.

o   After prolonged discussions with the military authorities, Maciej Dymny, a WiP participant from Szczecin, was allowed to fulfill his alternative military service by working in his home town, where he has been employed as a tram engineer since February 5, 1987. Nevertheless, the local draft board denied similar applications by two other WiP supporters -- Maciej Romaniuk and Wojciech Tadajewski -- on the grounds that only men with health problems were permitted to do alternative service. Tadajewski, however, was sent to work in a factory as a form of civil defense and is not required to live in a barracks.[10]

Alternative service often involves working in the coal mines, a practice which WiP finds absolutely unacceptable for two

81

reasons: 1) because WiP considers it immoral to force conscripts into a choice of " army, coalmine, prison;" and 2) because no legal regulations provide for work in coalmines as a form of alternative service. WiP is striving for changes in the conscription regulations themselves as well as in the accepted practices to ensure a humanitarian conscription process in Poland.[11]

The Polish government has actively sought to repress the WiP movement. The following measures have been taken against WiP activists:

o   The first to be jailed for refusing to take the military oath was 21-year-old Marek Adamkiewicz of Szczecin. Drafted on September 4, 1984, he refused to take the military oath in October of that year. On November 17, he was arrested under Article 305 of the Polish Penal Code and, on December 8, 1984, he was sentenced to 2-1/2 years of imprisonment. Adamkiewicz was released in August 1986 as part of the July amnesty, after serving more than two-thirds of his sentence.

o   On December 23, 1985, Wojciech Jankowski, a 21-year-old teacher from Gdansk, was sentenced under Article 231 ("persistent evasion of military service") to 3-1/2 years of imprisonment for refusing to serve in the military or to undertake military training. When he was not released during the September 1986 amnesty, Jankowski began a hunger strike in prison. He was released in early October 1986.

o   On February 12, 1986, Tomasz Wacko from Wroclaw and Jaroslaw Wojewodzki from Gorzow were arrested and sentenced to 1-1/2 years and 2-1/2 years of imprisonment, respectively. Wacko was released in August 1986; Wojewodzki was released in September 1986.

o　　On February 19, 1986, Jacek Czaputowicz, age 30, and Piotr Niemczyk, age 24, were arrested on charges of "founding and directing an illegal organization known as 'Wolnosc i Pokoj [Freedom and Peace],' cooperating with representatives of foreign organizations and intending to harm Poland's interests" (Art. 276 and 132 of the Polish Penal Code). They faced up to ten years in prison, but were released in September 1986 as part of the amnesty. International peace petitions supporting Czaputowicz and Niemczyk attracted over 4,000 signatures.

o　　On April 5, 1986, Krzysztof Sobolewski from Gorzow was arrested for refusing to take the military oath and sentenced to three years in prison. He was released in August 1986.

o　　On May 5, 1986, Jaroslaw Nakielski from Warsaw was arrested on charges of "persistent avoidance of military service." He was sent to a psychiatric hospital for observation, but escaped. On September 15 (after the amnesty), he voluntarily reported to a military attorney and was arrested. Nakielski was released on October 20.

o　　On June 14, 1986, Waclaw Giermek from Wroclaw was arrested for refusing to take the military oath. He was sentenced to two years of imprisonment, later reduced to one year.

o　　On November 24, 1986, Wojciech Hetman refused to take the military oath. The authorities sent him to a special military unit where he suffered many forms of harassment, including denial of correspondence and family visits, and assignments to the most difficult work.

o   On March 12, 1987, police in Gdansk searched the apartments of two WiP activists and detained three members of WiP. A peace activist from Boston who was with the activists was ordered to leave the country and the peace literature she had in her possession was confiscated. The day before the searches, all three had participated in a meeting to protest the construction of a nuclear power plant at Zarnowiec.[12]

After the amnesty in July and September 1986 for political prisoners in Poland, two WiP activists -- Jankowski and Nakielski -- remained in prison. WiP gathered over 10,000 signatures and organized demonstrations of behalf of the imprisoned activists. Jankowski was released on October 4; Nakielski was released on October 20. The fact that WiP activists were included in the amnesty was significant for the movement, for it signalled that they were considered to be political prisoners -- a status for which they had struggled since the movement was formed.

WiP activists are frequently subjected to fines for their actions, usually 50,000 zlotys (more than twice the average monthly salary). The general WiP principle, however, is not to pay such fines. As of this writing, the authorities have not taken further actions -- such as confiscating property -- in order to collect the fines. Actions for which WiP members have been fined include the following:

o   On July 3, 1986, WiP members commemorated the

40th anniversary of the start of a Jewish pogrom in Kielce. The participants were detained and given fines of 20,000 zlotys.

o   On December 6, 1986, in Gdansk, WiP staged a demonstration in support of the Jehovah's Witnesses imprisoned for conscientious objection. Nine of the participants were fined 50,000 zl.

o   On January 15, 1987, Malgorzata Gorczewska, a Gdansk Medical Academy librarian, was fined 50,000 zlotys for keeping illegal literature -- including WiP's translation of the Amnesty International newsletter -- with the intent to distribute it and foment public unrest. Wojciech Jankowski and A. Michalowski tried to attend her hearing but were detained briefly by police.[13] Amnesty International wrote to the Polish authorities to protest the persecution of those possessing AI materials.[14]

Many activists have been detained for 48-hour periods, during which time the authorities are not required to press charges against them.

WiP's campaign for the right to alternative military service has contributed to a change in the government's posture, if not in its outright position. On January 7, 1987, the army newspaper Zolnierz Wolnosci published an article with information about ways to apply for conscientious objector status.[15]

It should be noted, however, that on February 21, 1987, the official Soviet newspaper Izvestia published a strong attack on WiP. In addition to blaming the Western press for telling "the whole world about it," the article stated:

And what do you think such a group of young deserters would christen itself? 'Freedom and Peace.' No more, no less. In our time, who is going to listen to you if you're against peace and freedom? So they're dressing up in attractive -- albeit somebody else's -- clothes. As for the claim that this group is an 'organization,' its members are clearly indulging in wishful thinking.[16]

More ominous developments took place in the summer of 1987. In June, a defense ministry spokesman attacked WiP, claiming that it served hostile foreign governments by engaging in subversive activities aimed at undermining Poland's defense system. In July, August and September, three conscientious objectors were sentenced to prison terms of up to two years. These cases marked the first time since the 1986 amnesty that opposition activists were imprisoned in Poland, and could signal a change in the government's tactics in dealing with conscientious objectors.[17]

o   On July 23, 1987, Piotr Rozycki, a 23-year-old WiP activist, was sentenced to two years of imprisonment by a military court in Bydgoszcz for refusing military service. At his trial, Rozycki stated that "for moral reasons," he refused to perform military or civil defense duty, and he demanded the right to alternative, community service. WiP has been campaigning on Rozycki's behalf since his arrest in June.

o   On August 7, 1987, another conscientious objector -- Oskar Kacperek -- was sentenced to two years of imprisonment for refusing to take the military oath.

o   On September 7, 1987, Maciej Wijas was sentenced to one year of imprisonment in Wroclaw on charges of desertion, although he claimed to have deserted because of the mistreatment and discrimination he claimed to have suffered in the military. Wijas had been in prison since December 1986, when he turned himself in to the authorities. Wijas was released from prison the day after his trial -- on September 8 -- on the grounds that prisoners are eligible for release after they have served two-thirds of their sentence.

Certain practices of the military came to light at Wijas's trial. His allegations of mistreatment were supported in the court by the revelation that disciplinary actions had been taken against one of his superiors in the army.

o   According to reports by Associated Press and Reuters several dozen Jehovah's Witnesses are currently in jail pending trial on similar charges.

The Seminar

In a daring initiative, WiP held an open seminar from May 7-9, 1987, entitled "International Peace and the Helsinki Agreement." The most significant fact about the seminar was that it actually took place -- right in the middle of Warsaw -- and that peace and human rights activists from 17 countries of East and West (Austria, Belgium, Canada, Czechoslovakia, Denmark, Finland, France, Great Britain, Holland, Italy,

Norway, Poland, Sweden, Switzerland, the United States, West Germany and Yugoslavia) were able to gather to discuss issues of common concern. Over 200 people attended the seminar, including about 100 WiP activists, approximately 65 foreigners and roughly 50 other Poles (from Solidarity, the parish, etc.) WiP's seminar was the largest, independent, grass-roots peace forum ever to be held in the Soviet bloc, and the first to be truly successful (similar efforts in Moscow and Budapest were either broken up by the authorities or sparsely attended).

Not surprisingly, the authorities tried to prevent the seminar from taking place. Twenty-two WiP activists from some eight cities around the country were arrested en route to the seminar, in addition to six members of rural Solidarity. The authorities also tried to prevent the main organizers from around the country from attending the seminar. Those who were able to evade detention went into hiding and used circuitous routes to reach Warsaw. Several WiP activists who were detained for 48 hours (under Polish law, anyone can be detained without charges for up to 48 hours) arrived at the seminar on the third and last day. Government harassment against those planning to attend the seminar took the following forms:

o   Jacek Czaputowicz, the principal organizer, stayed in the Church for the five days preceding the seminar so as to evade arrest. On May 26, 1987, Czaputowicz was fined 50,000 zlotys by a misdemeanor court in Warsaw in connection with the seminar. He was found guilty of taking action intended to cause public unrest, publishing materials without a permit and participating in an illegal organization. Czaputowicz said he would appeal the verdict.

o   Gwido Zlatkes, a WiP activist, was detained but not released or charged after 48 hours. He began a hunger strike to protest his unlawful detention and was ultimately released after 100 hours. He was given a standing ovation when he arrived at the seminar.

o   Approximately 20 Westerners who listed the seminar on their visa applications as the purpose of their visit were denied visas. Among those denied visas were peace activists from Holland, Italy, Great Britain, Denmark and Finland.

o   Herbert Ruitenbery from Holland was turned back after he arrived at the Warsaw airport. Professor Hoffmann-Ostendorf from Austria was turned back on a train when he reached the Czechoslovak-Polish border.

After the initial obstacles, the authorities made no further attempts to obstruct the proceedings. Apparently, the authorities were surprised at the number of Westerners who came for the seminar and, perhaps in the interest of public relations, did not want to alienate the Western peace movement and Western public opinion in general. Presentations were made by representatives of WiP, Solidarity, the Church, several Western peace activists and representatives from Charter 77 in Czechoslovakia and the Ljubljana peace group in Yugoslavia. The participants discussed four central themes: peace and human rights; new detente; Otto Schimek and personal responsibility; and ecology.

It is important to note that the seminar was held in a Church, signaling the power of the Catholic Church in Poland and underscoring the impossibility of conducting such an

89

independent event outside Church grounds. However, of the four churches that had been effectively reserved for the seminar, three backed out the day before the seminar was to open, due to a letter from the Episcopate stating that political events cannot be held in a sacred place.

Given the different perspectives and mistrust that have often characterized the relationship between independent peace movements of the East and of the West, the dialogue that was fostered by the seminar was also of importance. This is due, in part, to another characteristic of WiP; unlike many civil rights movements in East bloc countries, it is willing to entertain the notion that no nation or superpower is an ultimate guarantor of freedom and human rights, and that it may not be necessary to be "pro-American" or "pro-Reagan" to be "anti-Soviet."

Environmental Concerns

In recent years, the terrible state of the environment in Poland, especially in the wake of the disaster at Chernobyl, has become an issue of increasing urgency. In an article that appeared in the July-August 1987 issue of The Sciences, Jean Pierre Lasota gives a chilling account of the environmental devastation in Poland:

Being downwind of the Chernobyl explosion was only the latest in a string of misfortunes in a country in which environmental devastation has become a feature of everyday life. According to government reports (many of which are not intended for public distribution), air, water and soil pollution are so hazardous in Poland that the health of at least one third of the country's population is at risk; that is, roughly thirteen million people now living there are likely to acquire environmentally induced cancers, respiratory disases, or a host of other illnesses. In most major cities, air pollution is fifty times higher than the established limits allow. Water quality is declining so rapidly that within the next few years the nation's entire supply -- rivers, lakes, and wells -- may be unfit for any use, including industrial. And as much as one quarter of the country's soil is too contaminated for safe farming.[18]

Even the official press, which is usually reluctant to provide information about the ecological destruction caused by industry, recently reported some disturbing developments. According to an official scouts' journal, as of 1987 there are no longer any forests in Poland that are not contaminated and several national parks have reported substantial destruction of the standing timber. Other government-controlled publications recently admitted that in some communities of Silesia, Poland's main industrial area, 90 percent of the children suffer from chronic respiratory conditions and that life expectancy there is three years lower than the average in other parts of the country.[19]

Given the severity of this situation, the population is becoming more informed about the hazards that surround them. WiP believes that this increased awareness should be coupled with increased pressure on the authorities in the form of ecological actions. WiP's concern with the environment is an important facet of its work. In its program documents, WiP discusses its position:

> Threatened with the ruin of the biosphere, pollution of air, water and soil, we realize that freedom should also be the possibility to live in non-devastated natural surroundings. At present, natural resources are wasted and the short-sighted policy of the authorities is destroying nature irrevocably. This is mostly due to industry which tries to save money by not installing the necessary equipment guarding against pollution. Thoughtless management leads to emaciation of the soil and disappearance of forests and waters.
>
> Freedom and Peace will strive for full information on the devastation of the natural environment.[20]

WiP was at the forefront of the massive response in Poland to the Chernobyl disaster. It was one of the first groups in Eastern Europe to stage demonstrations after the accident, and has conducted a campaign against a nuclear plant being built at Zarnowiec, about 40 kilometers from Gdansk (which has been nicknamed "Zarnobyl"). Other demonstrations have been organized to protest the construction of a second nuclear plant near Poznan.

o   On May 2, 1986, WiP groups in Krakow and Wroclaw organized demonstrations protesting the lack of information being provided about the Chernobyl accident.

Some 2,000 people took part in the Krakow march.

o   In Bialystok, an area most exposed to Chernobyl, about 3,000 people signed a petition calling for the suspension of construction of Poland's first nuclear plant in Zarnowiec, which is to be built with Soviet assistance.

According to WiP, the report of a governmental committee established in May 1986 to examine the construction of the Zarnowiec reactors found significant inadequacies with regard to staff training and the construction of the reactors. In its bulletin, WiP quotes a disturbing passage from the committee's report: "It should be stated that not all the demands related to the attainment of quality control have been secured. ..."

Another important target of WiP actions was the Siechnice steel mill near Wroclaw, which releases ferrochromium composites. Though not the worst environmental polluter in Poland, the steel works are harmful to the Wroclaw area, particularly with regard to the supply of drinking water. WiP activists in Wroclaw staged three demonstrations demanding the closing of the foundry -- on November 28, 1986, December 10, 1986, and January 10, 1987. The latter two protests were interrupted by the police and fines were levied against the participants.

The WiP activists who participated in the January 10 demonstration (which was broken up by the police before the planned march could begin), signed the following statement:

1. We believe our action concerning the Siechnice Steelworks to be valid and in the public interest. The use of police force against us, and our subsequent

prosecution before a Petty Offenses court is more proof that the authorities' concern for environmental protection is empty sloganeering.

2. At present the Petty Offences courts are used as a political weapon against independent opinions and not as an instrument of the rule of law. Presiding magistrates at the Petty Offenses courts are notorious for their ignorance of the law, assisted in this regard with false testimony by prosecution witnesses.

3. Therefore we cannot accept as valid the fines imposed and refuse to pay. We appeal to all, particularly to lawyers, to put public pressure on Petty Offenses courts to abide by the rule of law.[21]

On January 29, 1987, the Provincial National Council in Wroclaw announced that the Siechnice foundry would be closed before the end of 1992. WiP's campaign against the foundry, combined with the efforts of a range of official journalists and scientists, undoubtedly contributed to the authorities' decision to close it down, and is considered to be one of the movement's principal accomplishments to date. It is interesting to note that on February 21, 1987, the Polish Ecological Club voted to ask the municipal authorities in Wroclaw to pay the WiP fines resulting from the action.[22]

The way in which WiP targeted the Siechnice steel mill is typical of its step-by-step approach toward change. As Marek Krukowski, a WiP activist in Wroclaw, told The Washington Post:

This is an issue that people are just becoming aware of. There are at least 500 plants like this that are

94

causing serious damage and must be controlled. The only solution is for society to organize on the local level to attack the hazards one by one.[23]

The WiP group in Krakow staged demonstrations on March 27, 1987, protesting the environmental damage being caused by the Nowa Huta Steelworks. In leaflets distributed at the demonstrations, WiP appealed to the mayor of Krakow to close two chemical plants. Eleven people were detained, including Artur Kielasik, who was fined 50,000 zlotys and 30,000 zlotys for damages. Other participants were summoned to appear before tribunals.[24]

Though WiP is well aware that many of its potential constituencies are afraid of the costs they may have to pay for taking part in independent initiatives, and that therefore it is unlikely to develop into a mass movement, it believes it has an important part to play in altering the consciousness of Polish society. It has already succeeded in injecting the issues of peace and ecology into public discourse (and not in the sterile fashion with which these issues have been dealt in government propaganda), and it is broadening its effort to include discussion of international human rights. Equally important, WiP is renewing awareness in Polish society that individuals can influence the government to change its policies.

The fact that 20 conscientious objectors are not in prison, the closing of the Siechnice steel mill, and the holding of the seminar demonstrate that WiP is having an effect. Schooled in the experience of Solidarity and fueled by its own energy and determination, WiP is enlarging the space for independent initiative and, thereby, for the establishment of a pluralistic society.

Notes -- Poland

[1] Reprinted in <u>Peace and Democracy News</u>, Campaign for Peace and Democracy East/West, New York, September-October 1985.

[2] "Giving Real Life to the Helsinki Accords," European Network for East-West Dialogue. Berlin: 1987.

[3] <u>Peace and Democracy News</u>, op. cit., Summer-Fall 1986.

[4] <u>Peace and Democracy News</u>, op. cit., Fall 1986.

[5] David Warszawski, <u>Wolnosc i Pokoj - Szczecin</u>, No. 1.

[6] Jacek Czaputowicz, <u>Biuletyn WiP</u>, Warsaw, No. 2.

[7] "Freedom and Peace: A Conversation with Piotr Niemczyk on the day after his release from prison," <u>East European Reporter</u>, Vol. 2, No. 3, 1987.

[8] Polish Helsinki Committee, <u>Human Rights Violations in Poland 1983-1986</u>. New York: U.S. Helsinki Watch Committee, p.41.

[9] Piotr Niemczyk, <u>Biuletyn WiP</u>, Warsaw No. 1.

[10] <u>Uncensored Poland</u>, No. 8/87. London: Information Centre for Polish Affairs, April 1987.

[11] Uncensored Poland, op. cit., No. 5/87, March 1987.

[12] Uncensored Poland, op. cit., No. 8/87, April 1987.

[13] Ibid.

[14] Uncensored Poland, op. cit., 9/1987, May 1987.

[15] Franek Michalski, "WiPing Poland Into Shape," The Nation, May 23, 1987.

[16] Reprinted in: The Current Digest of the Soviet Press, No. 8, 1987.

[17] Jean Pierre Lasota, The Sciences, July-August 1987.

[18] Na Przelaj, 1987/17.

[19] Peace and Democracy News, Summer-Fall 1986.

[20] Uncensored Poland, op. cit., No. 5/87, March 1987.

[21] Ibid.

[22] Jackson Diehl, "Chernobyl Awakens Polish Opposition," The Washington Post, March 16, 1987.

[23] Uncensored Poland, op. cit., No. 9/87, May 1987.

V. USSR

Chernobyl became the tragedy that united East and West. In spreading throughout the whole world, radiation lifted the "iron curtain," because international efforts were required to eliminate the effects of the disaster. -- Moscow Trust Group, April 1987, "We Vote to Review Nuclear Power Programs"

The Soviet Union has been both a victim of foreign invasion and a perpetrator of external aggression in its purported quest for national security. The Soviet Union lost 20 million citizens during World War II. War memorials scattered throughout the cities and towns bear testimony to the devastation and suffering of the Soviet people. Almost every night, Soviet television broadcasts films about The Great Patriotic War, as World War II is known in Russia, along with frequent documentaries about the strength of the Soviet armed forces. Literature, theater and art continue to reflect a national preoccupation with the war.

In effect, World War II has been institutionalized in Soviet society as a means of consolidating the population around the government's foreign policy and peace proposals. It has become almost a cliche to say that the Soviet people do not want another war because they have already suffered so much in the last one. The Russian word for peace, mir -- which also means world (and which once meant peasant community) -- crops up on many propaganda posters throughout the country. The government has always tried to portray itself as a defender and promoter of peace, and to propagandize socialism as a system that preserves peace by its nature -- against incursions from aggressive imperialism which sometimes have to be fought in a "just war"

99

for the sake of preserving that peace.

In the countries of Eastern Europe, whose histories have been quite different from the history of the Soviet Union, and which have been victims of Soviet imperialism, usurpation of the word "peace" in communist government propaganda and policies has led to wide-spread cynicism among ordinary people about the meaning of the word and the usefulness of peace meetings and activities in general. In the Soviet Union, history and the memories of war have left such an imprint that the government's use of the word is still widely supported by the population at large. The official Soviet Committee for the Defense of Peace [SCDP],[1] a government agency, claims to have rallied 90 million contributors or members -- the entire adult working population of the Soviet Union -- and thus taps into a well-spring of popular sentiment. For many workers, ruble contributions to the Soviet Peace Fund are routine nuisances. On pay day, accountants present employees with a list of official committees for "voluntary contributions," and if a worker does not check off a box for a contribution, the blank space next to his or her name will attract suspicion. On the other hand, some intellectuals who may read Solzhenitsyn and criticize the Soviet regime bitterly make generous contributions of a day's wages or month's bonus to the Soviet Peace Fund in the belief that this helps to commemorate the losses of the war and strengthen peace. They do not seem to make the link between their peace sentiments and waging modern war; supporting "nationalist liberation" movements, for example, is an openly stated goal of the SCDP.

When Soviet propagandists boast that the Peace Committee is supported by individual donations, and point to the

100

grandmothers bringing in their deceased war veteran husbands' gold watches to contribute, they are telling the truth. But the other side of the coin is that because the hierarchic rule of the Communist Party permeates Soviet society at every level, and because information is controlled, it is easy to mobilize millions of people instantaneously behind the government's peace cause. Willing participants in a government-generated mass movement should not be mistaken for spontaneity or individual initiative and a sense of responsibility for the arm's race. Often, when Westerners ask Soviets if they are involved in the peace movement, they answer in surprise that their contribution to peace is "just doing my job -- the government takes care of it." A Soviet man may proudly show his Soviet army reserve card: peace needs to be defended.

Despite the general population's yearning for peace and memories of the terrors of war, the Soviet government has provoked widespread mistrust at home and abroad not only because of its foreign adventures, such as the war in Afghanistan, but because of its war against its own people. Stalin's purge victims totalled as many as those killed in the war. The repression of the civil rights movement in the 1960s and 1970s and the silencing of critics such as Andrei Sakharov, who was exiled to Gorky when he condemned the invasion of Afghanistan, have been cited as violations of international human rights agreements that raise the question of Soviet adherence to arms control agreements. The intense secrecy and closed nature of Soviet society has been considered a threat to world peace. Although the *glasnost*[2] or public disclosure campaign has dealt candidly with domestic social ills and has made real gains in extending the limits of public criticism, military and foreign policy matters have mainly been untouched. The military budget is not published, for example, nor subject to public debate. The numbers and types of troops and military bases at home and abroad are not publicized. When events like the invasion of Afghanistan, the shooting down of the Korean airliner, and the Chernobyl nuclear accident occur, the Soviet public is usually the last to know the truth, and is certainly not involved in the decision-making in the first place.

There are a number of signs that these factors are changing under the leadership of Mikhail Gorbachev. In April 1986, the Chernobyl accident became the first major test of Gorbachev's *glasnost* campaign. Sweden reported alarmingly high levels of radioactivity before the Soviet government officially admitted the accident two days afterwards -- when it was too late for public safety measures. But when officials began to deal with Chernobyl, it was with a much greater degree of openness than had ever been the case under previous Soviet regimes.

After the Chernobyl accident came more releases of political prisoners (Anatoly Shcharansky was released in February 1986, but dozens more followed after May 1986), the return of Andrei Sakharov to Moscow and to his position at the Academy of Sciences, and a Supreme Soviet decree to begin the review and release of political prisoners in earnest. By July 1987 about 215 political prisoners, or about 25 percent of the known cases, were released before the end of their terms. The lifting of some limits on the press for criticism of domestic issues raises hopes for increased tolerance of discussion of war and peace issues.

There have been a few indicators that lead in this direction. Alexander Bovin, writing in Moscow News (a Russian and foreign-language publication mainly meant for Western consumption but with significant readership in Russian among the intelligentsia) was the first to hint at the question of the actual defense necessity of the Soviet SS20 missiles in Europe; namely, if they could be so easily scrapped as the "double-zero option," an agreement to remove all intermediate-range nuclear missiles from Europe, seemed to be reaching a conclusion. Yevgeny Primakov of the prestigious Institute of the World Economy and International Relations, and said to be a close associate of Gorbachev, has recently gone on record as repudiating the Soviet doctrine of the export of world revolution,[3] long cited as evidence of the Soviet Union's sinister intent to dominate the world by force. But the declarations of "new thinking" by Soviet leaders have still to be tested by performance on the world scene and genuine efforts to institutionalize and put into law the recent measures aimed at liberalizing society.

Since Gorbachev's *glasnost* campaign went into full swing and political prisoners began to be released in batches in January 1987, unofficial groups have once again sprung up in various cities throughout the Soviet Union. Some are groups reconstituted with veteran dissidents and ex-political prisoners, and some are made up of young people not previously involved in dissent. *Glasnost* and a moratorium of sorts on political trials in Moscow and Leningrad since September 1986 have meant that such groups enjoy relative freedom from harassment and imprisonment. However, the arrest of religious believers in the provinces and forcible induction of conscientious objectors into the Soviet army continue, as do short-term detentions and beatings of demonstrators.

As never before, the peace issue has become the province of

103

every unofficial group to emerge; human rights, religious, nationalist self-determination and other activists have eloquently portrayed the ways in which their concerns are related to social and world peace. In recent months, for example, for the first time the Soviet Union's Hare Krishna movement, which has been heavily persecuted, held a conference and a press meeting, where it called for religious believers to unite their efforts in the peace movement. And a group of long-time Jewish refusenik scientists prohibited from leaving the Soviet Union because of alleged exposure to state secrets, have pointed out that the Soviet Union's outdated notions of an imminent threat of war used to justify restrictions on freedom of movement, and its contention that many citizens are exposed to information that could constitute a potential threat to the Soviet state, are in fact concepts that are an obstacle to peace. "A new approach to the question of trust and arms control should, logically speaking, involve a reappraisal by both sides of their concepts of national security."[4]

Among the most dramatic indications of a possible greater tolerance for non-aligned, independent peace expression have been the opportunities for independent peace activists to speak at official forums. These include an unprecedented presentation in May 1987 at an international peace meeting in Moscow, and another meeting in July 1987 when groups of peace, civil rights, and religious activists addressed an audience of 230 American peace activists who had joined with 200 Soviet members of the official Soviet peace committee for a walk from Leningrad to Moscow. The current climate under the *glasnost* campaign coupled with vigorous lobbying by visiting foreign peace activists made these meetings possible.

These victories have been balanced by defeats. Independent

104

activists now face a more subtle kind of political warfare by the regime, which uses a variety of dishonest propaganda techniques to silence unofficial opinion as thoroughly as if it had packed the activists off to the Gulag. A vivid example was this summer's effort by Soviet officials at the European Nuclear Disarmament Convention in England to portray a Soviet woman on the official SCDP delegation as a representative of the independent peace group, when in fact the real representatives of the group were forced to remain at home, blocked from obtaining exit visas.[5]

Andrei Sakharov

Dr. Andrei Sakharov, physicist and human rights campaigner, has been described as the only independent and authorative voice in the Soviet Union on disarmament issues. Sakharov, inventor of the Soviet H-bomb, was the first to advocate a ban on nuclear testing in three environments in the 1960s. After he denounced the invasion of Afghanistan in January 1980, he was apprehended and forcibly moved into exile in Gorky, 250 miles outside of Moscow, without trial or sentence. There, he was brutally silenced and mistreated, held in complete isolation and filmed openly by KGB cameras 24 hours a day. In December 1986, after a phone call from General Secretary Gorbachev to their Gorky apartment, Dr. Sakharov and his wife, Yelena Bonner, returned to Moscow and resumed residence there. The end of the couple's exile and their reinstatement in Moscow was widely greeted in the Soviet Union and abroad as the first concrete sign of Gorbachev's intentions to open up Soviet society. Dr. Sakharov was invited back to work at the Institute of Theoretical Physics and later accepted an invitation from the Soviet Academy of Sciences to work with the organizing committee of a major international peace conference in February attended by more than 900 foreign celebrities, scientists, writers and artists. Sakharov spoke for 10 minutes at one session of the conference saying that progress in human rights is essential to nuclear arms reduction. He called for freedom of speech, travel and emigration, and praised Gorbachev for advocating greater openness and releasing some political prisoners. Since his release, Dr. Sakharov has generally been supportive of Gorbachev's efforts, and stated in early 1987: "It's not right to say that it's only propaganda or window-dressing. Objectively, something real is happening. How far it's going to go is a complicated question. But I myself have decided that the situation is changed."

Dr. Sakharov was a controversial figure for both the Soviet government and the Western peace movement when he advocated the use of the American MX missile program as a regrettably necessary bargaining chip in the face of the Soviet arms build-up. This led the government and the Soviet scientific establishment to accuse Dr. Sakharov wrongly of desiring to encourage a U.S. nuclear attack on the Soviet Union. Now that, since his release, Dr. Sakharov has spoken against the SDI or "Star Wars" program, he has been reinstated in the favor of both the Soviet government and the Western peace movement. His criticism of a U.S. arms program has prompted some critics to conclude that he has been compromised by the Soviet government or forced to join a chorus of Soviet peace initiatives in exchange for his freedom. But it is important to understand Dr. Sakharov as a loyal opposition -- neither the leader of a dissident movement nor a tool of the regime -- who always, unequivocally, has spoken his mind freely -- even when it cost him terrible personal privation. Sakharov has long been a member of the Soviet scientific elite, and even in Gorky exile, retained his membership in the Academy of Sciences. He does not identify himself with the independent peace movement within the Soviet Union, and as an advocate of nuclear power, he has not been associated with the environmental movement. Recently, Sakharov proposed the idea of placing nuclear reactors underground to make them more safe.[5]/[6]

The Moscow Trust Group

Five years after its founding, the Moscow Group to Establish Trust Between East and West still survives. The Moscow Trust Group, as the independent peace committee is known, is one of the few non-official organizations in the Soviet Union that was able to keep above ground during the difficult years following the Soviet invasion of Afghanistan and the break-down of detente. Somehow, it has managed to keep afloat despite internal and external pressures, and has survived a succession of four Soviet leaders. Most other public dissident organizations during that period -- human rights monitoring committees, free-trade union associations, writers clubs, unofficial religious groups, and Marxist reform groups -- were disbanded under threat of arrest or were forced underground.

Founded in June 1982 by eleven scientists and other intellectuals in Moscow, the Trust Group has gone through a number of changes of personnel and tactics in the arduous five years of its struggle to gain recognition from the government and the Western peace movements. Initially, the Group called for the establishment of trust "between the USSR and the USA," but it developed ties with Western European peace groups and broadened its agenda and, in 1985, it changed its name to "Group to Establish Trust Between East and West." The original Trust Group founders and supporters were a coalition of scientists from the city of Moscow and the suburb of Dolgoprudny, many of whom were Jewish refuseniks. They were joined by young artists and writers from the alternative culture and "hippie" movements. One of the driving forces behind the merging of various types of people with differing experience was a young artist, Sergei Batovrin, who, as the son of a diplomat employed at the United Nations, had lived in New York for a number of years and spoke fluent English. Batovrin suffered forced psychiatric detention and constant police harassment before he emigrated to New York in 1983, where he continued to work on behalf of his colleagues. After they were released from labor camps and their situation became more tolerable, he began to pursue his art work. Batovrin was the one who designed the Trust Group's badge, a dove intertwined with the international peace sign, and many of the Group's slogans. He was known for popularizing the saying "Little Brother is Watching Back!" -- the independent movement's reponse to the Orwellian "Big Brother is Watching You."

The Trust Group has never established a leader or a strict political program, preferring to keep the door open for discussion with people of varying political or religious persuasions to create a permanent base for a non-aligned peace movement to grow in the Soviet Union. Eventually, the scientists from the suburb of Dolgoprudny withdrew from the Trust Group and established their own group and related seminars; other Moscow scientists remained in the Trust Group. Young people in the alternative cultural movements stayed in touch with the Trust Group, attending its seminars and sometimes becoming members while pursuing other activities.

In its founding appeal, signed by several hundred Soviet citizens, the Trust Group called for the abolition of nuclear weapons East and West, and the establishment of a "four-sided dialogue" where both the publics and governments of the U.S. and the USSR would participate, "enjoying equal rights" with the politicians in the armaments decision-making process. The Group and its supporters have drafted dozens of proposals for confidence-building measures between East and West, including exchanges of school-children, television "bridges," where Soviet and American citizens would speak before audiences in each other's countries, joint scientific and medical research projects, and the transfer of military funds to social needs and development in the Third World. Through a variety of creative tactics, they have made it possible for both Soviet citizens and visiting foreigners to see the complexity of the war/peace issue in the Soviet Union, and thus provide an alternative to one-sided official peace propaganda that blames only the West for the threat of war.

Among the peace actions staged by the Trust Group over the years are the planting of peace gardens; a demonstration in front of the British Embassy on behalf of women arrested for civil disobedience at the military base at Greenham Common; passing out of folded paper "peace cranes" and leaflets urging Soviets to write to Americans to establish personal friendships; displays of Western peace literature, posters, buttons and stickers, as well as their own hand-made buttons proclaiming that "Mutual Trust

Will Disarm the World"; passing out of booklets on radiation at the time of the Chernobyl disaster; and an annual international "ten minutes of silence" joined by activists from around the world.

Under the restrictive conditions that prevailed before the summer of 1987, when KGB presence and pressure was constant, the Trust Group did what was possible: they met and talked in their apartments and occasionally ventured out on the streets with posters and signature campaigns. This seemingly innocuous and ineffectual activity is put into context when we understand that the Trust Group provided a tremendous service: a clearing-house for independent discussion for Soviets and foreigners during a period when nothing could be done. Hundreds of young people from all over the Soviet Union, many of them on the young people's hippie circuit known as "The System," made their way to Trust Group meetings and spread their buttons and literature and ideas in their home towns. For visiting foreigners, most of whom are naive or uninformed about Soviet society, they provided a rough-and-ready glimpse of the sides of Soviet reality hidden from official life: the cruelty of secret police oppression, at the one extreme, and the warmth, passion and hospitality of Russian culture at the other.

Because they do not see themselves as a political organization, the Trust Group and its supporters have tended to refrain from comment about disarmament proposals made by the Soviet Union and the United States. Rather, in promoting the guarantees of the Helsinki Accords for the free flow of information and people, the independent peace movement sees itself as creating a space where an exchange of views can take place between ordinary citizens of the Soviet Union and the West

110

outside their respective political systems. The activists see the fostering of wide-spread grass-roots contacts and an increase in the openness of Soviet society as a fundamental requirement for peace, without which disarmament negotiations are doomed to fail.

Western peace movements, usually focused specifically on anti-nuclear weapons protest, were puzzled and frustrated by what they saw was a lack of focus by the Soviet peace activists, at the same time that they were impressed by official Soviet peace proposals initiatives such as a unilateral ban on nuclear testing. But like the other independent peace activists of Eastern Europe, the contribution the Soviet pacifists had to make was in searching for ways to bridge the gulf of the cold war and to get at the roots of the arms race: the hostility engendered by clashing ideologies and social systems, the oppression of human rights, the stereotypes of enemy images. They do not believe that weapons will ever be removed if the nature of the relations between the two superpowers are not changed, and if restrictions on the Soviet public's freedom of expression and freedom of movement continue. These restrictions threaten international security, since they enable a government to act without public oversight and control.

Generally, the Trust Group has been forced to maintain a cautious agenda and has avoided outright criticism of Soviet nuclear weapons policies because this would be considered tantamount to revealing military secrets or subverting the defense of the USSR--acts that are ruthlessly punished. The Group has steered away from criticism of weapon systems, not wanting to seem an adjunct to the one-sided platforms of the government. Though they do not want to be unbalanced, they cannot, for

111

example, endanger themselves by criticizing SDI and, at the same time, criticizing the Soviet Union's development of a similar system. Such criticism--even under Gorbachev--is viewed as an intrusion on the government's monopoly of defense information and policy.

Although the Group's founding appeal and statements seemed benign, differing little from the pronouncements of Leonid Brezhnev and later Soviet leaders, they were drafted carefully and cleverly. While Westerners may have been mystified by the significance of their content, the authorities understood what was "anti-Soviet" about them. In Moscow, at trials of pacifists and in attacks against them in the press, the substance of their documents and peace work was never addressed; rather, they were charged with trumped-up, unrelated "crimes." Most likely, officials feared the backlash in the West if they were seen to be persecuting citizens who took their peace propaganda at face value.

However, a provincial court commission far away from Moscow and foreign attention did use the Group's founding appeal to condemn an activist to a labor camp sentence, thus unwittingly exposing the government's attitude to home-grown pacifism. The official commission's evaluation spoke volumes about the government's aggressive co-optation of the peace issue and assertion that only the Communist Party was blameless in the arms race and was a force for peace.

The activist, Aleksandr Shatravka, 36, was one of the first signers of the Trust Group's founding appeal and was the only person to be tried for the Group's peace activity per se. A former victim of forced psychiatric confinement after an attempt to flee the Soviet Union in 1974, Shatravka was arrested in July

112

1982 and sentenced to three years of labor camp for circulating the Trust Group's petition in a forestry work site in Siberia where he was employed as a seasonal laborer. The workers had at first signed the appeal enthusiastically and arranged discussions on the peace and trust theme, but under KGB pressure after Shatravka's arrest, many withdrew their names. At least one worker was prosecuted.

Party legal experts in Tyumenskaya oblast at the Ural State University and the Law Department of the Rudenko Institute pronounced the Trust Group appeal "slanderous" because it purportedly circumvented the Party to appeal directly to ordinary Soviet and American citizens to work for peace and establish independent international groups -- thus calling into question the efficacy of the Party's peace efforts. The appeal was also "slanderous" for laying equal blame on the Soviet Union and the United States for the arms race, purveying "the well-known thesis of Western propaganda concerning the equal responsibility of imperialist and socialist countries for the cold war."

The Trust Group's spontaneous nature and lack of credentials was almost as irritating to the authorities. The appeal "could give rise to incorrect ideas, especially among that part of the population which is not well-prepared politically." Such politically-unprepared people should leave the job of disarmament to the specialists:

> The appeal to unite social forces in a struggle for peace is a harmful cosmopolitan doctrine...The call to unite international social groups is nothing other than a call for the formation of a group of "initiators" outside the framework of our state...The authors of

the appeal slander the actual policy of the USSR, the government of the USSR, and the leadership of the Communist Party of the Soviet Union, when they declare that "it is completely clear that politicians on both sides are incapable in the near future of reaching an agreement on any noteworthy reduction of arms; they are even more incapable of reaching an agreement on substantial disarmament"...The outward orientation is a weakening of the position of Soviet diplomacy in the negotiations in progress, to the detriment of the authority of the Soviet leadership in the eyes of those international forces which are considered by us, and can be practically used as, an effective reserve in the anti-imperialist and anti-militarist struggle....[7]

The last line was seen as a particularly sinister sign of the Soviet government's intentions with regard to the Western peace movements.

In 1984, letters addressed to Western peace activists from Shatravka reached the West describing his suffering in a labor camp in Dzhanatas, Dzhambulskaya oblast, which included repeated beating and mistreatment, long hours of forced labor and lack of medical care and nourishment:

> Since my arrest, those who work in the Procurator's office and investigative agencies, workers in hospital isolation wards, professors in the Serbsky Institute of Forensic Psychiatry, and now workers in the correctional labor camp, often ask me the same

questions: "Why do you do such work? Do you really think that our Party and government give too little attention to the problems of preserving peace and controlling the arms race?" Yes, they pay attention to these problems, but I cannot concede that the defense of peace is only a matter for the leaders of the State.

In February 1985, Shatravka was sentenced to an additional two years of labor camp on fabricated charges of possession of narcotics, planted on him by fellow inmates cooperating with the authorities. Shatravka was transferred to a labor camp in Gurev, Kazakhstan, then moved to Talgar Special Psychiatric Hospital, shortly before his release in June 1986 and subsequent resettlement in the United States in July 1986.

Aside from Shatravka, the Moscow Trust Group has suffered the trial and sentencing of five of its members to labor camp or exile: Larissa Chukayeva, two years labor camp, June 1986; Sergei Svetushkin, one year labor camp, January 1987; Vladimir Brodsky, three years labor camp, August 1985; Olga Medvedkova, two-and-a half years labor camp suspended, March 1984; and Oleg Radzinsky, five years exile, October 1983. Sergei Svetushkin was kept in prison for six months, re-tried, and sentenced to the period already served. He was released in May 1987 and remains in Moscow. Larissa Chukayeva was amnestied in December 1986 and remains in Moscow. Moscow authorities refuse to give her custody of her son. Vladimir Brodsky was released from labor camp early and permitted to emigrate to Israel in September 1986. Olga Medvedkova's sentence was lifted during the amnesty of 1985, and she and her husband, Yury, were granted exit visas in September 1986; they settled in the

United States. Oleg Radzinsky served some time in exile, but was eventually permitted to return to Moscow after acknowledging his guilt under pressure from the authorities. He emigrated to Australia in 1987.

In addition to formal trials and sentences, activists have been harassed in a variety of ways. Their phones have been disconnected, their mail has been confiscated, they are followed and have ascertained that their apartments are bugged. Dozens of group members and supporters have frequently been subjected to 15-day jail terms on false charges of "petty hooliganism"; short-term psychiatric detention; house arrest; etc. On December 1, 1986, for example, a day that was celebrated by Western groups such as the War Resisters League as a day to demonstrate in defense of jailed peace activists, there were 7 members of the Trust Group under various types of short- and long-term detention, and 7 under house arrest. The women who went out on the street that day with posters about their jailed husbands and colleagues were themselves detained.

In most cases, harassment of independent peace and environmental activists stops short of sentencing and jailing. The technique seems to be to jail leaders for 15 days at a time and to threaten students interested in the movement in order to thwart its influence. This is particularly true when foreign peace delegations are in town, or when other international events related to disarmament occur. For example, one round-up of Moscow peace activists occurred the same day that the Soviet Union pulled out of arms control talks in Geneva. Similarly, during the International Youth Festival in July 1985, the 27th Party Congress in February 1986, and the Goodwill Games in July 1986, young activists were sentenced to 15-day jail sentences or placed in psychiatric hospitals to prevent them from contacting foreigners or holding demonstrations. And in July 1987, during the American-Soviet Peace Walk, seven Trust Group members who travelled to Leningrad to try to hook up with the march were detained and sent back to Moscow, they were later able to meet with the marchers in Moscow.

The following is a selective chronicle of some of the incidents of persecution of the Trust Group in the last two years:

o   On December 3, 1985, four plainclothes KGB agents, accompanied by Nikolai Khramov's father, a member of the official Soviet Writers' Union, broke into a seminar of the Trust Group and tried to disrupt the meeting. They were surprised to discover that foreigners were in attendance, but refused to allow their remarks in Russian to be translated for them. In an emotional and angry interchange, the men shouted that "18-year-olds should not be allowed to discuss politics -- take them back to their parents." With regard to Soviet defense, they exclaimed "we're not surrounded, we can strike first if we have to."

o   On January 7, 1986, 18-year-old Irena Pankratova, who had joined the Trust Group in the fall of 1985, was detained and forcibly placed in Psychiatric Hospital No. 14. She had previously been detained twice, once on December 8 for the John Lennon rally, and again on December 10, for Human Rights Day. Pankratova's incarceration was similar to that of Olga Kabanova and Natalya Akulyonok, two high-school seniors active in the peace group who were put in psychiatric detention before

117

the Moscow International Youth Festival in the summer of 1985. They were released after an international protest campaign by Western peace activists. Pankratova was released after a month.

o   Annetta Fadayeva, of Leningrad, was detained on January 28, 1986, and placed in Psychiatric Hospital No. 15. She had participated in the John Lennon demonstration and other independent peace actions, including the signing of a petition to declare Leningrad a nuclear-free zone. She was returned to Leningrad, held in Skortsov-Stepanov Psychiatric Hospital, and was released in May 1986, suffering from the effects of heavy medication, including sulphazine and aminazine.

o   Right before the opening of the 27th Communist Party Congress, sixteen members of the Moscow Trust Group were detained on February 4, 1986, on their way to a meeting at the home of Group members Yury and Olga Medvedkov. Most were released after interrogation at police stations, but several activists were beaten severely and others were placed in psychiatric hospitals or handed 15-day jail sentences. Three were informed that they must leave the Soviet Union before February 16 or face imprisonment.

The peace activists were en route to their weekly meeting, where they planned to discuss a letter on peace issues they wanted to send to the 27th Communist Party Congress. The letter dealt in part with General Secretary Gorbachev's proposals to eliminate nuclear weapons by the year 2000, and stressed that efforts to establish free exchanges among ordinary people were essential for

118

peace. The detentions were apparently the worst crackdown against the group since its inception in June 1982, involved the largest number of activists to date, and combined all the types of repression used against the Group in recent years.

-- Viktor Smirnov, 35, a Trust Group supporter and leader of Moscow's counter-culture movement, was detained and interrogated, then sent to Belye Stolby, a psychiatric facility outside Moscow. Smirnov was previously detained in the summer of 1985 during the Moscow International Youth Festival. Smirnov was released briefly, then returned to psychiatric confinement in April 1986, and eventually released in 1987. He had previously been jailed without trial during the 1980 Moscow Olympics, and had spent a total of four years in psychiatric hospitals for his counter-culture activities. Smirnov has once again resumed his peace and cultural activity, and is one of the regular signers of petitions in Moscow.

-- Pavel Timonin, a Pentecostal activist and member of the Trust Group, and Aleksei Zveryev, Trust Group supporter, were taken to a militia precinct and sentenced to 15 days for allegedly resisting officers. Nina Kovalenko, artist, was detained and beaten to unconsciousness. She was subsequently hospitalized in Botkinskaya Hospital for trauma victims.

-- Larissa Chukayeva and Georgy Samoylovich, a Trust Group member, and two new members, Gutman Levitan and Veniamin Puzankov, were taken to a police station and questioned for four hours. Afterwards, at midnight,

119

they were forcibly put into a truck, taken to the woods on the outskirts of Moscow, beaten severely, and left in the snow. They managed to make their way back to Moscow early in the morning. Nikolai Khramov, 22, was forcibly taken to a truck where a high-ranking KGB official told him that he had two days to pick up an exit visa and leave the Soviet Union or face imprisonment. He flatly refused the offer and was threatened with arrest. Khramov had never applied to leave the Soviet Union and remains in Moscow.

-- On September 2, 1986, militia and plainclothes agents broke into a Trust Group seminar at the apartment of Trust Group member Anna Nelidova and checked the documents of all those present. Three members were arrested: Nikolai Khramov, Sergei Svetushkin and Aleksei Zaitsev. They were sentenced to 15 days of jail, and all declared a hunger strike. Khramov was hospitalized briefly and released at the end of his term. Zaitsev, who refused to drink water, was released on September 9.

o   In February 1987, during an international officially-sponsored peace forum, three members of the Trust Group tried to display posters with their name and peace symbols in front of the Central Exhibition Hall, opposite the Kremlin, Their demonstration lasted only seconds; their posters were ripped from their hands and torn up. Uniformed and plainclothes police then took the activists inside the building for questioning, and they were released.

After the accident at the Chernobyl nuclear power plant in April 1986, the Moscow Trust Group and other, similar groups become more active in environmental demonstrations. For the first time, activists took a position directly critical of Soviet policy by demanding a rapid and full account of the Chernobyl disaster and its consequences, and calling for the abolition of nuclear power. In seminars, demonstrations and leaflets, the Trust Group disseminated information on the effects of radiation on health and the food chain. Apparently as a consequence of the Group's increased activism, and a desire by the Soviet government to make a public relations gesture in the aftermath of severe criticism of the handling of the accident in Western Europe, two of the Group's political prisoners were released in 1986 and permitted to depart for the West, and five others were granted permission to emigrate.[9]

Other peace and environmental protests staged include the following:

o   On May 20, 1986, Moscow Trust Group activists held an anti-nuclear demonstration near Vakhtangov Theater on Arbat Street. This was the first known public demonstration against the use of nuclear energy in the USSR. The activists carried signs bearing such slogans as "Atoms Can Never Be Peaceful," and "We Vote for Reconsideration of Nuclear Energy Policy on This Planet." Prior to the Chernobyl disaster, the Group's activity on this issue had been limited to educational seminars and a proposal to the U.S. and Soviet governments to establish international safety norms for the storage and production of nuclear materials. Twelve Group members were arrested by the KGB on their way to the demonstration. Three who made it to the theater were detained by the militia. All of those detained, with the exception of Larissa Chukayeva, were released.

o   On May 31, 1986, the activists repeated their anti-nuclear demonstration at the entrance to Gorky Park. Eighteen activists were arrested by KGB and militia after collecting the signatures of dozens of passers-by to an appeal calling for reconsideration of nuclear energy policy. The detainees were released after three hours.

o   Two Americans, Anne-Marie Hendrickson, 29, and Robert McGlynn, 30, of New York, demonstrated in Gorky Park on August 3, 1986, with Trust Group member Nina Kovalenko. The activists carried a sign saying "Peace and Envrionmental Safety for All. No More Hiroshimas and No More Chernobyls," and passed out leaflets on the effects of radiation. They were detained by the militia for one hour, then permitted to leave the country without incident. Several British citizens and Trust Group members demonstrated again the following week. They were encircled by KGB and militia, but permitted to hand out leaflets on preventative health measures after exposure to radiation, which were snatched up by eager passers-by.

o   Twenty demonstrators came to the Arbat mall on April 26, 1987, the first anniversary of the Chernobyl tragedy, carrying banners that said "Chernobyl Must Never Be Repeated" and "Ensure Safety in Nuclear Power." They called on passers-by to sign their posters in support. Many people complied, with both vocal and

122

written support, and the demonstration proceeded without trouble until foreign correspondents and TV crews arrived. Groups of plainclothesmen who apparently had been watching the demonstration quickly appeared on the scene and stopped the TV filming by knocking an NBC TV camera to the ground. Senior police officers in uniform watched but refused to intervene. The protesters were pushed and led away, and five were taken to a nearby police station for questioning and document checks.[10]

On the same day, in a separate, but also spontaneous event, thousands of Soviet citizens travelled to Mitinskoye Cemetary and filed silently past the graves of 26 victims of the Chernobyl disaster.

Twenty-two members of the Moscow Trust Group (including three of those sentenced) have been allowed to emigrate: some of them had applied to leave and been refused in the past; others had not applied to leave and were unexpectedly given exit visas.[11]

After four of the Group's chief spokespersons -- Yury and Olga Medvedkov and Vladimir and Dina Brodsky -- left the Soviet Union in September 1986, the Group was thrown somewhat into disarray. As their friends departed, three Group members were put into 15-day lock-up after the KGB broke up a weekly seminar meeting. One of them, Sergei Svetushkin, was arrested and later tried on trumped-up charges. After the departure of the Medvedkovs -- internationally known geographers who spoke fluent English, had extensive contacts in the Western peace movement, and frequently hosted the Trust

123

Group meetings in their apartment in the southwest of Moscow -- the peace activists in Moscow, especially those who had recently become involved, lost both direct contacts to the West and continuity with the history and experience of the Group. Western peace activists, hundreds of whom had regularly visited the Trust Group over the years and had kept it supplied with literature and moral support, now had to hunt down new addresses and try to speak Russian. The new members of the Group's coordinating committee, who did not speak English, organized a group of translators to help them maintain communication with the foreigners.

By December, a splinter group was discussing disbanding the Trust Group, saying that it had lost credibility since so many had departed for the West, and that since a national organization was not possible, it was better to leave peace to the government. Without the consent of the majority, several individuals issued a statement of disbanding to Western wire services. The majority quickly released a counter statement, signed by 20 people, denying the Group's closing and re-emphasizing its decision to continue its activity despite official harassment.[12] They held a number of meetings on the topic of the education of children and the militarization of society, and released a lengthy document on the subject.

Eventually, the Trust Group recovered from the blow and replaced its losses with new activists. It maintained a core membership of about 15-30, with a constantly shifting group of an additional 75-100 who regularly attend seminars. Most of the founding members, who were mainly Jewish refusenik scientists, have been permitted to emigrate. The large number of members who have emigrated have prompted many critics of the Group to charge that they have engaged in peace activities as a route to rapid emigration. But they respond that in the USSR, generally, the people who are willing to risk independent activity are those who feel they have nothing to lose, since they have already been ostracized for applying to leave. Westerners are sometimes puzzled when Soviet citizens desire to leave their homeland; they have difficulty understanding life in a society where foreign travel and freedom of expression have generally been impossible for the average intellectual who is not part of the nomenclatura, or official elite.[13]

New members of the Trust Group include Jewish refuseniks, other scientists and professionals, Pentecostal and other religious activists, and young people from the alternative culture and "hippie" movements. Despite KGB surveillance, the group holds weekly peace seminars in various apartments in Moscow, frequently stages demonstrations, gathers signatures to peace petitions, distributes literature, and meets with Western peace activists visiting Moscow and Leningrad.

In the spring of 1987, the Group began to renew its energies, and started discussions of a new declaration of principles (see Appendix IV), given the rapidly changing political situation in the USSR and new opportunities for increased freedom of expression. Political prisoners were beginning to be released and were making their way back to Moscow; they were naturally attracted to the Trust Group's meetings. (In fact, some of them, such as mathematician Vadim Yankov and worker Vladimir Gershuni had hastened their impending arrests back in 1982 when they signed the founding appeal of the Trust Group, and authorities grew alarmed at the rapid coalitions being formed between veteran civil rights activists and new peace activists.)

125

Some of the ex-political prisoners formed a new study group called Democracy and Humanism to examine the histories of the Soviet Union and the United States. The veteran activists, who included Valeriya Novodvorskaya of SMOT, the free-trade union group, asked the Trust Group members and supporters to join them. Some Trust Group people were apparently reluctant to join an openly political and human rights group when it was unclear how this would be viewed by the authorities. Eventually, several of the most politically-seasoned of the Trust Group members, who had been involved in human rights groups in the past, signed the first declaration of Democracy and Humanism, which called for a complete amnesty and rehabilition of prisoners of conscience, complete freedom of circulation of ideas, publications and people regardless of frontiers (specifically, making Western publications available to the general public in the USSR), and other planks of the civil rights agenda of the 1960s and 1970s. The Democracy and Humanism seminar was eventually placed under the wing of the Trust Group, although a majority of the members did not openly support it, and it remained autonomous. It is likely that the SCDP's demand of the Trust Group that it disassociate itself from Democracy and Humanism only reinforced the protective ties between the the two groups.

For the first time, in drafting the new principles, the Trust Group dealt openly with human rights issues and the war in Afghanistan: "We are in principle opposed to the presence of foreign troops in foreign territories, first of all, the presence of Soviet troops in Afghanistan." The group re-emphasized its commitment to "cooperate closely with activists in the peace movements abroad in order to overcome the mistrust towards the

126

peoples of the USSR both in the West and in the Third World and in countries allied with the USSR" and to "oppose the growing militarism of public consciousness."

We do not set as the goal of our activity the promotion of any government in winning for itself trust in the international arena, including the government of our own country. We believe that only the efforts of an independent society, of the ordinary peoples of the East and West, can guarantee the establishment of a climate of trust and a stable peace. Genuine detente is possible only from below, through the growth of a world-wide revolution of grass-roots peace initatives...[Human rights and peace], in our view, are inseparably linked. It is impossible to speak about peace without also discussing human rights issues. In the same way, it is unacceptable to be involved with the struggle for human rights while relegating to second place the problem of preserving peace, and ultimately, the survival of humankind....Peace in the world and peace in society depend on one another in the most intimate fashion. On the one hand, irreproachable observance by the authorities of human rights cannot help but have an impact on the elimination of mistrust in the international arena. The mistrust that is experienced towards a government that violates human rights is also extended towards ordinary citizens. Observance of these rights by governments will further the development of trust between peoples.

In addition to urging overall observance of the Soviet Constitution, the Group called for an amnesty of all prisoners of conscience; changes in Soviet legislation to prevent persecution of people for their convictions; abolition of the death penalty; and the "right to pacifism" or establishment of alternative civilian service for conscientious objectors; and freedom of travel and choice of residence through removing restrictions on emigration and repatriation and dismantling of the Soviet system of obligatory residence permits; and the free flow of information and ideas.

A third of the new principles was devoted to protection of the environment and conversion of military production to the peaceful needs of society. A review of current atomic energy programs and the shut-down of RMBK-type reactors [the Soviet acronymn for the design of the Chernobyl reactor] were urged.

On April 5, 1987, the Trust Group was able to hold its first large public meeting in a public hall, something it had never been permitted to do in the five years of its existence. Nikolai Khramov and Aleksandr Rubchenko spoke at a branch of the Central House of Architects before a conference of activists involved in a semi-official organization known as the Common Cause Conference, a club for Moscow intelligentsia interested in ecology, religion, and philosophy. About 200 people were in the audience, and their response was enthusiastic and positive. The two read the Group's new Declaration of Principles, spoke for about half an hour, and then answered numerous questions. Fifteen people endorsed the Declaration at the end of the meeting.

During this period, the Group began to make its first direct

128

contacts with East European peace activists. Before, such communication was carried on via travellers from the Western peace movement who were able to visit both the Soviet Union and East European countries and show the East bloc activists Western peace publications such as END Journal, Peace and Democracy News, and Across Frontiers that frequently reported about the Eastern movements and contained the full texts of their principle documents. A letter from the peace movement in Ljubljana, Yugoslavia, reached the Trust Group; the Ljubljana activists had written to the SCDP in defense of the Trust Group's persecuted members. The Trust Group members proceeded to lodge a protest with the Yugoslav Embassy in Moscow on behalf of six Slovenian conscious objectors standing trial. East German peace activists telephoned the Trust Group. The Polish Freedom and Peace Group sent the Trust Group an invitation to its May seminar in Warsaw. Although the Trust Group members were denied the opportunity to apply for the trip, they sent their greetings and solidarity and planned their own seminar about nuclear power during the same week.

In May 1987, at what has been described as a historic event not only for the independent peace movement, but for the Soviet Union, a representative of the Trust Group was permitted to speak freely at the Fourth Information Meeting-Dialogue sponsored by the SCDP. In February, Dr. Andrei Sakharov had been permitted to speak at an international peace forum, two months after his release from seven years in internal exile. But this was the first time that an independent grass-roots group, as opposed to an individual who is part of the elite, was permitted to be represented in an official context. Indeed, many observers considered it the first time since Stalin's era that an independent group's voice could be heard at an officially-sponsored event -- and on the issues that are the most sensitive for the government, namely, war and peace. Some 250 persons from around the world attended the forum, including activists from the U.S., Canada, Britain and Australia as well as many West European countries who had supported the beleaguered independent peace group since its inception in June 1982. After protests from Western peace activists that in the new atmosphere of *glasnost* independent activists should be allowed to speak, Irina Krivova, a spokesperson for the Trust Group, gave a 15-minute presentation on the group's activities to build trust at the grass-roots level between East and West, the obstruction of free expression on peace issues, the arrest and trial of member Sergei Svetushkin and the forcible drafting of members who are conscientious objectors.

More suprisingly, the event was covered in substantive manner in May 1987 by Moscow News in an article entitled "Right To Speak: Moscow Discusses the World's Future" and was mentioned, albeit in a disparaging aside, in Izvestiya. Moscow News noted that Julie Enslow of the American peace group Mobilization for Survival criticized the SCDP for not including the Trust Group in the international dialogue meeting. Vladimir Oryol, first vice-president of the SCDP, told Moscow News that the SCDP "didn't object" and that "all who sincerely wish to struggle for the survival of humankind and for the establishment of trust between the Soviet and other peoples are welcome into the Soviet peace movement," although it attacked the independent group's use of "foreign go-betweens" in attempting to gain entry to the meeting. (Over the years, the SCDP has studiously ignored all the letters and statements sent to it by the Trust Group, and in 1983, forced a Trust Group member to leave a meeting held at its offices in Moscow with Britain's Greenham Common women activists. Without the "foreign go-betweens," the SCDP would never have met with the Trust Group.)

In a samizdat report of the meeting entitled "Historic Moment or Disappointment?"[14/], the Trust Group described the behind-the-scenes efforts of the SCDP officers to hinder the participation of the Trust Group by creating a series of petty obstacles and attempting to get Krivova to submit her speech for approval. Her appearance at the meeting was largely due to pressure by foreign peace activists, and the SCDP apparently caved in as a tactical maneuver while the international meeting was underway. The Group concluded that although the event represented a historic victory, it was tempered by the fact that permission was still required to speak.

o   One positive outcome of the Trust Group speech may have been the release of Svetushkin on May 25. Svetushkin, a former Soviet diplomat active in the Trust Group who had been publicly critical of the handling of Chernobyl and the occupation of Afghanistan, was arrested last November and tried in January on trumped-up charges of "parasitism" and "non-payment of alimony." The parasitism charges were dropped but prosecution continued under the alimony charge, despite the fact that Svetushkin's ex-wife was not pressing charges and the payment had been sent. Svetushkin was re-tried and sentenced to the amount of time he had already served -- six months -- and allowed to return home. While in transit prison, Svetushkin complained of mistreatment and

131

pleaded to be moved to labor camp to serve his original one-year sentence. There has been speculation about psychological and physical pressure used against Svetushkin in prison, since after his release he was reported to be in poor health and was refusing to leave his home or to speak to his friends and colleagues.

On June 5, Krivova called a press conference to announce that negotiations were underway to gain a place for the Trust Group on the Soviet delegation to the European Nuclear Disarmament convention in Coventry in July 1987. The SCDP had hinted to visiting foreign peace leaders who inquired about their presence that this was a possibility, given the new atmosphere of *glasnost*. The press conference was attended by an SCDP official, a <u>Moscow News</u> correspondent, and Sergei Grigoryants, an ex-political prisoner who edits the independent journal called <u>Glasnost</u>. But late plans for the Trust Group presence were scuttled after the SCDP began to demand that the independent activists refrain from unspecified "anti-Soviet" statements and presented a list of ultimatums to the group, including disassociation from a new discussion group called Democracy and Humanism and unswerving adherence to the SCDP's own platform (which only denounced Western missiles).[15] Most discouraging, the SCDP refused to petition the visa office to grant a visa for the Trust Group's candidate for END, Yury Kiselyov; such an exit visa can only been granted when there is an officially recognized sponsoring organization.

The Group issued a statement on the SCDP's attempt to derail their participation in the END Convention, but the SCDP was not content to leave it at that. By the time the Convention

132

had opened on July 15, the official Soviet news agency TASS had a story on its wires that the original Trust Group had disbanded and that a "sub-group" member, Olga Sternik, was travelling with the official SCDP delegation to Coventry. Although the Trust Group immediately repudiated Sternik's representation, and Western peace activists alerted to the scam confronted Sternik and obtained an admission that she was not representating the Group, some Westerners were still left with the mistaken impression that, under *glasnost*, the Trust Group was allowed to travel and speak freely abroad. Although some Trust Group members said Sternik was collaborating with the KGB, others pointed out that KGB agent or not, she was not a "regular cadre" of the SCDP and as such, represented a step closer to actual independent people's representation at such international fora.

Conscious of its need to upgrade its negative image as an official agency promoting only Soviet foreign policy goals, the SCDP has assembled several officially-registered but purportedly grass-roots "public organizations" which reportedly accompanied them to Coventry. These were Rock Musicians for Peace and Green Peace (the English translation of Zelyony mir, not formally affiliated with the Western organization Greenpeace). According to Martin Walker of The Guardian [July 4, 1987], Rock Musicians for Peace was part of the newly-legalized Moscow Rock Club and had been formed "to persuade the suspicious Soviet cultural authorities that their participation [in a July 4 rock concert with American rock stars] would not embarrass the Kremlin."

On July 9, 1987, there was another "first" for the Trust Group: 16 members were permitted to speak in a public auditorium to a large audience of both Soviets and Americans at

133

the end of the Soviet-American Peace Walk. The American organizers of the Walk invited the Trust Group to speak, despite protests from the SCDP, to provide a look at Soviet dissent for the walkers. The event was filmed by both Soviet and American TV crews. Besides the Trust Group, a group of Jewish refuseniks and Hare Krishna representatives were also allowed to speak. The Soviets who took part in the walk, officers and members of the SCDP and others who were carefully selected by officials, were incensed, and, yelling and shouting, they engaged in heated debate with the Trust Group and the dissidents. One man said angrily, "I am against the people who want to leave our country." Surprisingly, it was an SCDP interpreter who agreed to translate for the Americans. The Trust Group presentation was only about 10 minutes, but they saw it as an important opportunity to express the fact that "Soviet people have no control of our foreign policy yet."[17]

Independent peace activity similar to that of the Moscow movement has been reported in the Russian cities of Leningrad, Gorky, and Novosibirsk; in the Ukrainian cities of Odessa and Kiev; and in the Baltic cities of Riga and Tallinn. Groups modelled after the Moscow Trust Group have been set up in these cities, but little information has reached the West of their activities other than the founding appeals circulated in 1982 and 1983. From the very beginning, the independent peace activists had difficulty in keeping track of their numbers because they were reluctant to keep membership lists that might be used as "hit lists" by the KGB if they were seized in routine apartment searches. The decentralized, amorphous nature of peace and ecology movements also makes it difficult to determine the numbers involved. The activists' estimates of those involved throughout the Soviet Union are 1,000 to 2,000 men and women, a figure which includes the core-group activists in each city who make their names public, those who have signed petitions circulated by the groups or who have attended events sponsored by them, plus supporters who do not reveal their names but take an active role. These numbers, although small by Western standards, represent a significant phenomenon in the Soviet Union, where mass independent movements continue to be discouraged by the authorities, and where independent links between cities are difficult to form.

Friendship and Dialogue

A group of physicists and other scientists from the Moscow suburb of Dolgoprudny, a city closed to foreigners and Russians because of classified research, have also continued a peace research seminar since January 1983, when they broke away from the Moscow Trust Group after extensive KGB persecution in order to continue their research more quietly. Recent reports indicate that the Dolgoprudny group, which now calls itself Friendship and Dialogue, has actively resumed discussion clubs in various apartments around Moscow, and is once again willing to receive foreign visitors. In addition to its Peace and Social Research Seminar, the Friendship and Dialogue Group founded a Round Table English Language Club and a Hebrew Conversation Club. Like the Trust Group, they recruited their lecture attenders from the Jewish refusenik intellectual milieu, and tried to provide activities attractive to their interests, because these were the people often most willing to take part in unofficial activity.

The Dolgoprudny scientists had been meeting sporadically since 1980 and five of them joined the Trust Group in 1982. (They were Viktor Blok and Boris Kalyuzhny, who emigrated to the United States in 1987, and Gennady Krochik, Igor Sobkov, and Yury Khronopulo, who remained in the USSR.)

In article for the first issue of Glasnost magazine, released in Moscow in July 1987, the Friendship and Dialogue Group wrote of its Peace and Social Research Seminar. The Seminar has no limitation on topics for discussion:

> The chief criterion for selecting papers to be read at the seminar is the social and generally humanitarian significance of a given issue. The seminar will strive to have its activity foster the raising of the level of people's independent thinking and social activity between ordinary people in the East and West, in order to strengthen democracy, trust and peace.

Among the 23 papers read in 1986 were: the reasons for the Chernobyl disaster; medical and biological consequences of the accident; "bottlenecks" in Soviet science; genetic consequences of environmental pollution; Phoenician culture; the history of the Decembrist Frolov; the activity of an American group called Independent Initiative; the social religious background of Hanukkah.

Like the Trust Group, the Friendship and Dialogue Group has emphasized that anti-weapons protests alone will not lead to peace because they do not tackle the reasons why the weapons are there in the first place. In a description of its work, presented in Glasnost, the Group wrote:

The conclusion of agreements on the reduction and limitation of arms can not be the only basis for peaceful coexistence among states with differing political and social systems. Clearly, we must strive to create an atmosphere of international trust by means of a rapprochement of cultures, based on spiritual values. Such an atmosphere, in reducing international tension, will in turn create additional motivations for disarmament. The activity of independent groups can play a substantial role in creating an atmosphere of trust.

The Dolgoprudny scientists had disagreed with the Moscow Trust Group activists about the program for an independent peace movement in the Soviet Union and the tactics to use. They were issues that face every peace group in the world, but were more critical for the Soviets because arrests and imprisonment were always brutal and long-term, not the brief arrests usually experienced by Western activists arrested for trespassing on military bases. The "civil disobedience" that the Soviet pacifists were speaking of was not in fact that, since their arrests came after they freely assembled and expressed themselves, rights purportedly guaranteed by the Soviet Constitution and international agreements to which the USSR is party. But freedom of expression and assembly is limited in theory by the Constitution to what is "in the interests of the people and in order to strengthen and develop the socialist system" (Art. 50) and in fact, is limited in practice by the KGB. Thus, street demonstrations and samizdat publications become a kind of "civil disobedience" against arbitrary state restrictions that some citizens agree to risk for the sake of their ideals and the human rights cause.

The Dolgoprudny scientists favored scientific research, discussion, self-education and public education, and withdrew from the public protest, demonstrations, and appeals that inevitably led to arrests, and the self-defense (the petitioning of state authorities, etc.) that ensued and became all-consuming. The Trust Group believed that public protests and direct action were the only responses given the urgency of problems like the arms race and the Chernobyl disaster, and were willing to risk job loss, police harassment, arrest, etc. in the pursuit of their cause. The questions of how much to raise civil rights questions and engage in self-defense were heatedly debated, and unfortunately, in the atmosphere of constant and intense KGB harassment, those who did not want to fight to the end were viewed as compromised.

Discussion Clubs

Since Gorbachev's *glasnost* campaign began, groups like the Dolgoprudny discussion groups have sprung up "like mushrooms in the rain," as the Russian saying goes. We know about Friendship and Dialogue because its members chose to risk contacts with foreigners. Although many people at institutes and enterprises have taken part in similar discussion clubs, they are invisible because they do not speak to Western travellers or the foreign press. One such group active even before Gorbachev came to power came to the attention of Western observers only when it was persecuted by the KGB:

138

o   In 1984, a group of young researchers at the Moscow Physical Engineering Institute (MIFI) were detained at their workplaces by KGB agents. The Institute prepares specialists in the field of applied military physics research. All students go through a security clearance in their first year in order to be admitted to classified research. Four detainees and their associates were accused of creating an unofficial group within the Institute's Komsomol (Young Communist League) and conducting independent studies in philosophy and peace. One of those detained had tried to make contact with a diplomat at the Indian Embassy and, through him, to contact peace organizations abroad. The scientists said they had been studying Soviet society from a Marxist perspective and opposed bureaucracy and corruption. The detainees reportedly withstood the KGB interrogation and insisted on continuing their activity. Komsomol leaders and a Moscow City Party Committee official in charge of counter-propaganda were assigned to "re-educate" the young scientists. No further reports on their activity have reached the West, but they seemed to be typical of the types of unofficial discussion clubs that have arisen within institutes.

More has begun to emerge about these types of clubs. The first issue of the samizdat journal <u>Glasnost</u> described their activities. <u>Glasnost</u> correspondents provided records of discussions at institutes like the Central Economics and Mathematics Institute of the Soviet Academy of Science (TSEMI),

139

where there are clubs called Perestroika [reorganization, the word used by Gorbachev for reform] and Social Initiative. Generally, the glasnost campaign has given them courage to come out of the woodwork, and allusions to their existence and some of their talk emerges in the official press through discussion of informal associations. Such clubs may also be officially inspired by the institutes' leaders to generate greater participation by the work force, which perestroika seeks.

The SCDP has responded to the challenge posed by the presence of the Trust Group and other independent peace and ecology groups with efforts to coopt them, or to create groups with the same names that are actually under their control. On June 4, 1987, for example, the fifth anniversary of the Trust Group, the official Soviet news agency TASS tried to overshadow the unofficial group's announcements by announcing the founding of a new officially-registered association called Zelyoni mir, which translates as Green Peace, which will apparently deal with environmental issues. When asked about the after-effects of Chernobyl at a meeting in Vienna in October 1986 sponsored by the International Peace Coordinating Committee, a group that links like-minded autonomous peace groups in Europe, officials of the SCDP claimed that a Green Club was permitted to exist. Moreover, students and young people were freely able to take positions for the abolition of nuclear power and publish newsletters at discussion groups within the Komsomol. When asked to produce citations of such publications, they implied that they were internal bulletins that were not available to the general public.

Representatives of the Trust Group, emigres Yury and Olga Medvedkov, who were also at the IPCC meeting, spoke of the persecution of anti-nuclear demonstrators in the wake of Chernobyl. They also mentioned that not long before their departure to the West, they were approached by members of the Green Club and asked to join them -- an effort to coopt the energies of the independent activists into officially-controlled channels. When the Medvedkovs asked whether criticism of Afghanistan and nuclear power would be encouraged in the Green Club, the answer was negative.

The tactic of co-optation rather than suppression is believed to be used increasingly with many types of clubs or associations around the USSR. A recent article on Soviet literature in Index on Censorship, which includes an interview with Leningrad poet Viktor Krivulin, describes the activities of Club 1981, a literary group in Leningrad about which little was known previously, but which has taken part in the historic preservation movement. It also sheds lights on the kinds of tactics the KGB and other authorities use in co-opting or channelling social initiatives that arise independently:

> Krivulin is one of the Leningrad poets who, six years ago, joined a group known as "Club 81". Or perhaps "joined" is too strong a word. "We were more or less forced into it," he explained. During the 1970s, he and many other writers had started publishing their work abroad. "We weren't prepared to compromise," Krivulin said....In Leningrad, he and other like-minded writers set up samizdat journals (37, The Northern Post) for their own work and translations of foreign poetry and philosophy. Periodically, they were subjected to searches or

hauled up for questioning. "But the KGB was beginning to change its tactics. They couldn't simply get rid of us -- we were too influential. Their aim was to try to accommodate us within the system. They wanted to find out who we were, what we were doing--give us a kind of official identity. That was the point of the Club. It was their idea, not ours."

The eventual outcome of that process was the publication, in 1985, of a selection of work by members of the "Club," Krivulin among them, under the title Krug ("Circle"). In view of the history he related, I was not surprised to find Krivulin less than enthusiastic about his first official publication. "They didn't really publish our work. They murdered it. A subtle form of murder, but murder all the same. They chose our least interesting work, and they published it in a context that was completely alien to it."[18]

The emergence of new groups, independent and semi-official, that may or may not be under official control, considerably muddies the political waters and makes it quite difficult to determine the degree of compromise that may be involved. But if official bodies are ever to be reinvigorated, and if a genuine civil society or public life is ever to arise in the USSR, there will inevitably be those individuals or organizations that must remain in the grey area between officialdom and independent initiative. This is bound to cause confusion and conflict until the former relinquishes its death-grip on society, and the latter carves out its identity and moves from negative opposition to positive contribution.

Baltic Republics

In the Baltic republics of Estonia, Latvia and Lithuania, the nationalist rights movements have part of their platforms a demand that the Baltic republics be part of any West European nuclear-free weapons zone. This demand is organically linked with the movement for self-determination in these republics -- which are occupied by Soviet forces and have suffered increasing "Russification" -- because the decisions about nuclear weaponry are made in Moscow. In December 1983, three Estonian human rights and peace campaigners who had signed the appeal calling for the nuclear-free zone were convicted of "anti-Soviet activity." Architect Lagle Parek, now 46, was sentenced to six years in labor camp and three years in internal exile. Her co-defendants, Heiki Ahonen, now 31, a geodetic engineer, and Arvo Pesti, 31, a philologist, each received terms of five years labor camp and five years exile. Other Estonians were warned in connection with this trial. Ints Calitis, 56, a plumber and jeweler from Riga who also advocated the nuclear-free zone, was arrested in April 1983 and sentenced to six years strict-regimen labor camp. He was released early in July 1986 after his name became more widely known when well-known ex-political prisoner Anatoly Shcharansky, who had been in labor camp with Calitis, began to speak of him. Starting in January 1987, the remaining Baltic prisoners began to be released by pardon or through the Supreme Soviet decrees that have released more than 215 political prisoners throughout the USSR.

In August 1986, demonstrations took place in Tallinn,

143

Estonia, organized by workers who resisted forcible assignment to the Chernobyl nuclear reactor to clean up radioactive debris. Several hundred workers were reportedly involved, and although many were detained, apparently all were released and no trials are to be held. The Soviet press subsequently denied the report, and several of the workers also disclaimed the demonstrations in statements for publication in the West. Those activists who speak out risk harsh government treatment:

o   Mikhail Bombin, 35, of Riga, is a leading activist in the independent peace movement in Latvia and a member of the Pokrovskoye Church choir. On November 13, 1984, he was detained on a train from Moscow after he spoke to a soldier and expressed his opinion that the war in Afghanistan should be stopped, and that it was a sin to take the military oath. He was searched and copies of the Herald of the Russian Christian Movement, published abroad in Russian, were confiscated, along with a prayer book and personal papers. In January 1985 he was summoned to the prosecutor's office and informed of a case against him on charges of "anti-Soviet slander" for distributing religious and peace literature and making statements. The basement of his church was also searched, and copies of George Orwell's 1984 and Russian Orthodox journals, along with personal correspondence, were seized. On December 16, 1985, Bombin was sent for psychiatric examination in Riga, and subsequently sent to the Serbsky Institute in Moscow where he was found mentally fit to stand trial. He was released to return to Riga in March 1986, and remained free until his trial. Bombin was tried in August 1986, and sentenced to two years of compulsory work outside Riga. In March 1987, he was released early from compulsory labor under a decree of the Supreme Soviet, and is currently living in Riga with his family.

The Hippies

Other independent groups, known as the "Group of Good Will" and "Independent Initiative," are involved in peace activity in Moscow, Leningrad, Riga, Tallinn and other cities all over the Soviet Union. They are a loose formation of students and young people who call themselves hippies [khippi] and describe their activity with a made-up Russian verb, khipovat'. They range in age from teenagers to some in their late 20s and 30s who, in the 1970s, when there was a surge of interest in youth culture and Western ideas and music, formed the Soviet hippie movement known as sistyema, "The System." At least several hundred young men resisted the draft at that time (mandatory for all able-bodied men at age 18) and were incarcerated in psychiatric hospitals; this kind of draft resistance, although barely publicized, continues. One of the chroniclers of the alternative movements, Nikolai Khramov, an independent samizdat journalist and photographer who is himself a Trust Group member and conscientious objector, writes of the hippie movement in a recent samizdat review of the movie "Is It Easy to Be Young?" which was the first public film treatment of unofficial youth culture (but which omitted the footage about hippies in the final version of the film.)

Unlike our punks and "heavy-metallists," which are no more than five or six years old as a phenomenon, the first hippies appeared in the Soviet Union right after they appeared in the West, at the end of the 1960s and the beginning of the 1970s...But it would be incorrect to say that they are simply an imitation of their Western peers. In my view, their emergence in our society was no less logical, and probably even more natural than in American society. But in America, it's rebellion against the bourgeois establishment; here, it's reaction to total state control, the suffocating domination of moribund dogma, and the origin of the Great Brezhnev Stagnation.

Those who were around at the beginnings of the "System" are now very much over 30. Some of them, of course, stopped "dropping out," and returned to society in one way or another. Some of them broke off from Soviet society completely and left the USSR on the wave of the "third emigration." Some of them drank themselves to death, and some of them got sucked into the quagmire of drugs. Some of them got into Christianity, like Aleksandr Ogorodnikov, the founder of the Christian Youth Seminar, who paid for this by serving almost nine years of labor camp. And some, taking the route of more conscious and purposeful protest, filled the ranks of the democratic movement: Yury Popov and Sergei Troyansky, founders of Free Initiative, the youth anti-war group, and Aleksandr Rubchenko, a member of the Moscow Trust Group and the Initiative Group for the Defense

146

of the Disabled in the USSR.

Soviet hippies did not cause a revolution in social consciousness. But the movement continues to exist, and its numbers are growing (of course, mainly in the big cities). The next generation, born at the end of the 1960s, shares the alternative philosophy of the hippies. Although they have been overshadowed in recent years by "metallists" and punks, the picture remains the same. Of course today's "System people" are not Western hippies and, most likely, not their Soviet predecessors of the beginning of the 1970s. But the name "hippie" has stuck, although most of them live at home, and, given the laws making "malicious rejection of socially-useful labor" a crime (Art. 209 of the Russian Criminal Code), they are forced to work. The authorities' treatment of them is the same as any other manifestations of youth non-conformism, and even more strict.

Khramov goes on to explain why the hippies are not shown in the film.

The protest of the hippies, in my view, is of a deeper and more conscious nature than the carnival and slap-stick high-jinks of the punks. It is the hippies who profess the ideology of pacifism, which is so desirable by the Soviet government for the Western countries and absolutely unacceptable in our own country, where it is declared a means of "concealing war preparedness, deceiving the masses and distracting

147

them from an active battle against imperialist wars" (<u>Great Soviet Encyclopedia</u>, 2nd edition, vol. 32, p. 251), since "in order to eliminate the inevitability of wars, as Leninism teaches, capitalism must be destroyed" (<u>ibid.</u>) It is precisely the hippies who are the fermenting brew for various non-conformist teachings, from Children of God to Zen Buddhists and Hare Krishna to more or less traditional Protestant sects. Consequently, the protest of the hippies is far more dangerous for the spiritual and ideological monopoly of the authorities in a totalitarian society than other manifestations of mass youth dissent.[19]

The fluctuation in police tactics in dealing with unofficial demonstrations in Moscow this year was illustrated by the brutal dispersal of a hippie pacifist art show.

o   On May 3, 1987, Moscow's hippies and punks gathered at Gogolevsky Boulevard, a green meridian near the center of town flanked by two statues of Gogol (one standing and triumphant, the other sitting and reflective), a popular hang-out for hippies, pacifists and counterculture activists. The artists displayed their religious, ecological and anti-militarist works by propping them on park benches. The show, which included works about Chernobyl, lasted about an hour and attracted many Soviet visitors as well as Western reporters. Police repeatedly told the young people to remove their art but it wasn't until two-and-a-half hours later, when foreign correspondents had left, that they took action. A police bus drove to the scene, and a large number of plainclothesmen, policemen and soldiers from the MVD (some of whom were drunk) charged the crowd, beating artists and passers-by and forcing them into the bus. The artists lay down on the ground in protest and were dragged to the bus by their arms, legs and hair. Anna Kamenskaya, a Moscow Trust Group activist, was kicked in the face by a woman uniformed police officer who grabbed her by the hair and beat her head against the bus. Arkady Kurov, 26, was beaten when he tried to defend his wife, Nadezhda, who was eight months pregnant, and who had fainted after being struck repeatedly as he watched. Nikolai Khramov, another Trust Group activist, was beaten by plainclothed agents who banged his head against the bus.

Seven artists were detained and taken to the police station. Six were released upon identification after three or four hours. Passports were confiscated from Vitaly Zyuzin, Anna Kamenskaya and Yekaterina Kashnikova, who were ordered to appear at the station the next day on charges of "petty hooliganism." Arkady Kurov was held overnight and threatened with criminal charges of "malicious insubordination to a police officer." But after Western correspondents inquired about him, he was fined only 50 rubles for "petty hooliganism" and released.

On May 4, plainclothed and uniformed police, including MVD troops, once again raided Gogolevsky Boulevard after young people gathered there. Police charged a crowd said to number about 250 people, arresting and striking both men and women, grabbing them by their hair and twisting their arms behind their backs. Some were dragged into a bus and beaten savagely with fists and sticks. The assailants put bags over their victims' heads to muffle their cries. Some were severely injured, including Yuliya Rimanov, 22, of Leningrad, who was placed in City Hospital no. 71 with facial fractures, and Fyodor Pakovich, 18, who was taken unconscious to the hospital after two policemen began to strangle him when he tried to take out his camera. Several others were said to have suffered broken ribs or other injuries including Konstantin Orlov, 18, the third to be hospitalized. The fate of one detainee, Maksim Stolpovsky, was not immediately known. Within two hours, about 60 were detained and taken to the police station. Several hours later, all were released except five who were held overnight and released the next day.

On May 10, 11 people went to stand at the foot of the Gogol statue on the Boulevard in a demonstration for peace and human rights. Activists unfurled banners demanding freedom of assembly and demonstration including one that said: "Remember the Helsinki Human Rights Charter!" and another that said "KGB and MVD! Protect Human Rights! Observe the Constitution! Respect the Dignity of the Individual!" Hundreds of passers-by were attracted and plainclothed and uniformed police mingled in the crowd and tried to provoke fights. For more than an hour, the demonstrators answered questions from a gathering crowd of citizens who openly sympathized with them. Then several men with military

150

bearing tore up some of the banners, crying "We spilled our blood for you!" Seeing the likelihood of physical assault, the demonstrators dispersed and went to the police station to pick up their passports (seized the previous day), carrying a human rights poster that had remained in one piece. On the way, they were attacked by people calling themselves members of the public who dragged them into the Fifth Precinct station. Three Trust Group members, Nikolai Khramov, Alexander Rubchenko and Sergei Yurlov, were detained, and Yurlov was beaten. At the station, their assailants, claming to be Afghan war veterans, cooperated with the police. In all, 14 were held by police for four hours, warned about severe punishment if they repeated such activity, and released.[20]

Surprisingly, the police brutality was covered by the official Soviet press, although two months after the incident. Komsomolskaya pravda, the newspaper of the official youth organization, the Komsomol, wrote on July 3, 1987, that dozens of hippies who had been loitering in a park were hauled off by police. Some were so severely beaten that they had to be hospitalized. The correspondent seemed to condemn the excesses, saying "The law provides equal protection for those with all sorts of haircuts, or with no haircut at all." Two days later, Moskovskaya pravda criticized the police for harassing and beating young motorcyclists, known as rockers.[21] It was not the first time that Afghan veterans were used to harass pacifists. Trust Group member Alexander Rubchenko wrote about such harassment in a samizdat article entitled "Not Only in Asia," where he illustrates the way in which one group of society,

151

young Afghan veterans hardened by the horrors of combat, are pitted by the authorities against another group of society, young men who avoid the draft or who are active in the pacifist movement. The Lyubery, the young toughs and body-builders that have recently been covered in the Soviet and Western press, have also been sicked on hippies and pacifists.

o   Activists Nikolai Khramov, 22, and Aleksandr Rubchenko, 25, were attacked on a street and beaten severely on May 9, 1986. It may have been orchestrated by the KGB to prevent the two peace movement leaders from organizing public protest against the Chernobyl accident. The assault was performed by five or six persons, under the direction of a certain Malikov, a graduate of a spetsnaz (special assignment) course at a military academy, who had been commissioned to Afghanistan. Ten other men stood by the attackers, and a KGB vehicle was spotted in the distance. Khramov had already filed legal charges against KGB agents who assaulted him on April 13 on his way home from a Trust Group seminar. On April 24, Khramov was summoned to the procurator's office, told to drop the charges and urged to sign a statement that he had no claims against the KGB. Curiously, the statement contained a truthful description of the assault, which is believed to be unprecedented in the history of the persecution of dissenters by the KGB. Khramov refused to sign the statement. In a further unprecedented development, the attackers were brought to trial in August 1986. Malikov was sentenced to two years of corrective labor without deprivation of freedom and a fine of 20 percent of his salary. Another man who had taken the least part in the beating was sentenced to three years of strict-regimen labor camp and a third was sentenced to two years in a reinforced-regimen labor camp.

Youth Groups

In the 1980s, in addition to hippies, Western-style punks and heavy metal rock music-lovers (known as metalisti) have also appeared and spread. Some are the children of the privileged elite, whose parents have access to Western goods and travel abroad. Others are working-class youth and are often under-employed in jobs like parking-lot attendants, security guards or street-sweepers. Under Gorbachev, rock groups and alternative music culture have spread like wild-fire and have forced the government to approve some of the more popular bands like Autograph and Aquarium which now play in officially-staged concerts in the Soviet Union and abroad.

Western rock music and clothing styles are not necessarily an indication of Western ideas of democracy, or of home-grown dissent, nor are rock and punk music and anti-war and ecology movements necessarily related; a young man can very easily serve in the Soviet Army (and most do) and still listen to Western music. Yet walking down the Arbat, the new shopping mall built in time for the 1985 International Youth Festival, a visitor is likely to spot groups of young people playing guitars and will be surprised by the frankness and dissent of their lyrics. All topics, including the war in Afghanistan, psychiatric oppression, and the damage of the environment are dealt with openly in the young people's songs. An advantage of music and song lyrics is that they are extremely portable. A group can set up a guitar session and disband it quickly if disapproving adults or police come by.

Even before Gorbachev, at the end of the Brezhnev era, youth groups arose that sometimes took more radical positions than the Trust Group in calling for resistance to draft and an end to the war in Afghanistan. Less is known about these groups than the Trust Group, because they have not actively sought out foreign contact; their members tend not to be highly educated and do not speak foreign languages so that visiting foreigners cannot communicate with them easily. They shun all official life and involvement with the state (for example, in such procedures as obtaining legal residence permits, obligatory in Moscow), and this sometimes extends to shunning contact with prominent dissidents and foreigners, perhaps to avoid undue attention from the authorities and ensure that their own activities, which mainly consist of unofficial rock concerts, poetry readings and art shows, will not be suppressed.

One such group, called Good Will, has taken as its hero the late Beatles singer John Lennon, and each year on December 8, the anniversary of his death, they stage peace demonstrations on Lenin Hills, sing Lennon's songs and carry peace posters. These demonstrations are broken up by the militia; dozens of young people are rounded up, and sometimes interned. In 1985, several young people ended up in psychiatric hospitals after John Lennon Day and were released several weeks later after receiving heavy medication. Reportedly, several dozen young pacifists are currently being held in psychiatric hospitals and prisons around Moscow for resisting the draft or taking part in demonstrations.

154

One youth leader, Yury Popov, was arrested in 1983 and charged with distributing leaflets calling for an end to the death penalty and the war in Afghanistan; he was subsequently accused of drug possession and is still being held, apparently in a psychiatric hospital. Because the use of drugs is prevalent in the counter-culture, it is easy to discredit any social activist with drug charges.

Another group, calling itself Free Initiative or Independent Initiative was founded in 1982 and periodically holds demonstrations and leafletting actions, denouncing the occupation of Afghanistan, calling for an end to the death penalty and to the compulsory draft, and urging grass roots contacts between peoples of the East and West. Periodically, the Independent Initiative activists hold demonstrations on Lenin Hills or travel to the Baltic republics where rallies of hippies and other young non-conformists are held. They, too, have been subject to government harassment.

o   Sergei Troyansky, 32, one of the founders of the youth anti-war movement called Independent Initiative, was arrested in his apartment at 9:00 a.m. on October 28, 1986. His arrest was preceded by a search, during which agents seized his typewriter, five copies of the Independent Initiative's brochure protesting the war in Afghanistan, Trust Group documents (although the groups are distinctly separate, there is some overlap and cooperation between the two), and a brochure from an Australian peace group called the Canberra Peacemakers entitled "Civil Defense," which was about nonviolent resistance against aggression. Troyansky was taken to the

Moscow prison Matrosskaya Tishina and charged with Art. 224, possession of narcotics. It is not known if drugs were found during the search, or if they were planted. The day after his arrest, officials once again searched Troyansky's home and found boots and clothes belonging to him that had traces of spray paint on them. This was grounds to charge him with spray-painting a number of slogans that appeared at the time on Moscow walls: "Stop the Shameful War in Afghanistan! Gorbachev--Murderer of Afghan Children!" and others.

At least one young man has taken more radical measures in protesting Soviet aggression abroad. In 1985, Tatyana Osipova, a member of the Moscow Helsinki Group who was jailed for her human rights monitoring activities, came across a young man in a prison convoy in 1985 named Leonid Gromov, who was 21 at the time. Gromov, who was employed at the Ulyanov Automobile Factory as a tool-and-die maker, committed arson at his factory when he found out that his factory was manufacturing armored vehicles that were being sent to Nicaragua and Afghanistan. He apparently discovered that foreign manufacturing patents, including some American patents, as well as French lathes, were in use at the factory. Gromov burned technical documentation in various offices over a period of time in order to hinder production at the factory. Authorities were so alarmed that Vitaly Fyodorchuk, the Minister of Internal Affairs, became personally involved in the affair. After hidden television cameras were installed at the plant, Gromov was caught, sent to the Serbsky Institute for Forensic Psychiatry, found insane, tried in absentia in December 1985 and sent to a special maximum-security psychiatric facility in Kazan. Two years later, reports indicate that Gromov has been continuously and heavily medicated and is depressed and lethargic.

Conscientious Objectors

Mandatory military training for boys and girls is included in all school curricula. The military draft is compulsory in the Soviet Union for able-bodied youths when they reach age 18. They generally spend at least two years in the armed forces. Those who are studying can defer the draft, but increasingly, young men are being taken out of universities or institutes after one or two years of study to fulfill their military service obligations. Evasion of the draft is thought to be widespread; even before the *glasnost* era, the Soviet press complained about young people avoiding draft through such subterfuges as frequent changes of address to elude the Voyenkomat, or draft board. The Soviet public was recently scandalized to read an expose in the press about members of the party and government elite who used their influence to keep their sons from being drafted or sent to Afghanistan.

Each year, a number of Soviet youths choose psychiatric detention or labor camp rather than serve in the army. A number of religious believers, such as Baptists, Jehovah's Witnesses, and Tolstoyans, refuse compulsory draft on the grounds of conscientious objection and are punished under laws governing evasion of compulsory military service (Art. 80, punishable by one to three years of imprisonment); evasion of training courses or draft registration (Art. 198-1, punishable by up to one year); and refusal to swear the military oath (Art. 249).

157

No status of conscientious objector is recognized by Soviet law, and there are no service programs as alternatives to the draft. Sometimes religious soldiers who do not take the military oath are not prosecuted, but transferred to construction units. But there is also evidence that religious believers who go into the armed forces and refuse to bear arms are sometimes brutally treated and subjected to frequent beatings. Several deaths have been reported in such cases.

Young men who seek to emigrate often wish to avoid the draft because reserve training or active military service may be construed as having access to military secrets, even if a soldier works in non-classified areas such as in military bands or social clubs. Emigration applicants are often denied visas on the grounds of past military service. Frequently, youths from families that have applied to emigrate are drafted into the army apparently for the purpose of preventing the family from leaving. The draft constitutes a form of persecution of such prospective emigrants.

Members of the Moscow Trust Group and related pacifist groups in the Soviet Union who have rejected the draft on grounds of conscientious objection have suffered psychiatric internment, imprisonment, and forcible drafting into the army. The draft is thus also used as an instrument of persecution against such outspoken individuals. At times, young people are drafted despite poor eyesight or health problems that would normally exempt them from military service, and draft resisters have been forced by the government to serve.

o   Dmitry Argunov, 19, a draft resister active in the Moscow Trust Group and the "punk" music movement, was forcibly abducted into the army in November 1985. Soviet police broke into his home in the morning and took him away to an unknown destination. As far as is known, his arrest is related to a November 9 action where he distributed leaflets on Moscow streets announcing that he was resisting the draft because of conscientious objection. On November 9, Argunov was scheduled to face a draft board commission and be inducted into the Soviet Army, but he refused to answer his summons and returned it with a statement explaining that he was refusing the draft because of his pacifist convictions. Argunov had been warned by the authorities for his participation in the Trust Group in the past. His whereabouts were not known until July 1986, when the address of his military unit became available. Under pressure, he had taken the military oath to serve in the army, rather than serve a labor camp sentence for refusal to bear arms.

o   Lev Krichevsky, born 1967, was forcibly drafted into the army on December 24, 1986. He had been active in the Moscow Trust Group, was a conscientious objector, and wishes to emigrate. Krichevsky has poor vision (he is legally blind in one eye) and had reportedly been exempted from military service on these health grounds in the past. But apparently his activity in the Trust Group caused the authorities to use the draft as a method of punishment. Because he refuses to do military service, he has been beaten constantly, has suffered kidney damage and has high arterial pressure. Medical care has been refused.

159

According to Trust Group supporters, the KGB and military officials have repeatedly held discussions with Krichevsky where, under threat of repression through the court system or detention in a psychiatric hospital and beatings in the barracks, he has been told to reject his pacifist convictions, leave the Trust Group and become a "normal soldier." When authorities failed to extract a declaration of the oath of allegiance to the Soviet military services through physical and psychological pressure, they placed Krichevsky in a hospital and gave him some type of heavy medication, so that, in a condition where he was not responsible for his actions, he signed the oath. After this event, his mail and packages were confiscated and through brutal beatings, authorities tried to get him to refuse visits from his parents and friends. He was denied the right to write letters and his whereabouts were concealed by the military even from his relatives.

o   In July 1984, Nikolai Khramov, at that time 20 years old, was jailed for 15 days for refusing a summons to the draft board for a medical examination. In August, he was arrested in his apartment and carried by KGB and police agents where he was held by his hair and beaten severely. He was sentenced to another 15-day term. On August 20, he was arrested for a third time, two days after being released from his previous terms. On October 24, Khramov was seized in the metro in the presence of friends from the Trust Group, three days before he was supposed to have presented himself at the draft board for induction. He was forcibly taken to the airport, and put on a plane to a military base in the Soviet Far East,

160

where he was arrested for resisting orders several days later. He was shunted from one facility to another, spending some time in a psychiatric hospital, until he was unexpectedly released from the army in March. When he was presented his release papers, he saw that they had been issued to take effect months before he was actually let go. Since the forcible drafting, Khramov has repeatedly suffered short-term detentions and beatings but is currently free and active in peace and unofficial cultural activities.

o   Serafim Yevsyukov, 26, was sentenced in 1980 to two-and-a-half years of labor camp for refusing to serve in the army. His family had been seeking emigration since 1978. In April 1986, he was rearrested in labor camp and sentenced in May 1986 in a closed trial in Domodedovo, outside Moscow. Yevsyukov's parents and sisters, as well as two foreign reporters, were not permitted in the courtroom. He was sentenced to an additional three years of strict-regimen labor camp. In July 1987, Yevsyukov was released early in connection with the 70th Anniversary of the Revolution amnesty, and he and his family emigrated to France.

o   Yevgeny Gette, born in 1966, a member of Jehovah's Witnesses, was sentenced in the Kirghiz SSR in 1986 for refusing to serve in the army. His term is not known, but since the maximum sentence is three years, he is not believed to be eligible for release until 1989. His name has not appeared on the lists of recently released political prisoners and his fate is not known.

o   Baptist Pavel Podznyakov, who was serving in the

161

army on Sakhalin Island, was tried for refusing to take the military oath. His sentence is not known. His parents were brought for questioning to the KGB and asked if their son had been mentally normal during childhood. His fate is not known.

o   Baptist Andrey Bill, born in 1965, of Nizhnyaya Ala-Archa, Kirghiz SSR, was arrested in December 1983 in the army for refusing to take the military oath. His sentence is not known.

o   Baptist Vyacheslav Minkov was drafted into the army in November 1982. He was moved from one division to another and beaten severely by other soldiers at each location. During the winter, he was ordered to stand outside all night despite a temperature of 40 degrees below zero. In April 1984, he was interned in a psychiatric hospital in Chernigov, Ukraine. The administration told his sister that he was considered schizophrenic because he kept "talking to God."

o   Yury Burda, 20, converted to Christianity after being drafted into the army. He began serving in May 1983 and refused to take the military oath. In October 1983, he died, reportedly by accidental electrocution. His family has questioned the circumstances of his death after examining his body and finding it mutilated in ways not consistent with an electric shock.

o   Aleksandr Yakir, 32, was sentenced to two years of labor camp in August 1984 for evading the draft. He is the son of refusenik activists Yevgeny and Rita Yakir, who have waited more than 12 years for permission to emigrate. Yevgeny was refused an exit visa on the

162

ground that his engineering work was secret, although it has been a decade since he was dismissed from his job and the information to which he had access is outdated. Yakir completed his sentence and returned to his parents. The family was eventually granted exit visas.

Ecology Groups

In July 1987, it was reported that the Moscow Trust Group had decided to create an ecology seminar within its group because there was a great deal of interest in environmental issues. At the seminar's first meeting, a speaker gave a report on the environmental threat posed to the Kotun river in the Altai mountains from a projected hydroelectric plant. In addition to flora and fauna, caves with ancient hieroglyphics were threatened with destruction.

Reports occasionally reach the West of other groups involved in independent study of disarmament and environmental issues, inspired by the example of the West German Green Party.

USSR News Brief, a biweekly bulletin of human rights news published by Russian emigre Dr. Cronid Lubarsky in Munich, reported in May 1987 [22] that a number of unofficial groups or "informal associations" as they are called in Russian, had emerged with varying programs, mainly focusing on ecology and the preservation of historical and cultural monuments. At least 300 people in Leningrad alone were said to be involved in the groups, the largest of which are Salvation, Peace, Ecology of Culture, and Cultural Democratic Movement. The four largest groups are united in a coordinating group called the Council of Ecology and Culture. The Council (soviet) tried to put its candidates in the election of local soviets on June 21, 1987. After their attempt to register their candidates was rejected because the organization itself was not officially registered, they announced a signature campaign to get their candidate, architect Aleksey Kovalyov of the Salvation group, on the ballot for elections to the Leningrad Party executive committee.

USSR News Briefs reported in July that in April 1987, the Council for the Ecology for Culture was renamed the council of the socio-cultural movement Epicenter. Nine "informal" or unofficial groups joined the council, which began to publish a monthly bulletin entitled Mercury, edited by E. Zelyonskaya. Although the publication has not formulated its profile yet, it hopes to inform its readers about the programs and activities calendars of various groups. In May, Epicenter changed its name to Cultural Democratic Movement and created a council, in which various groups had proportional representation. The council formed a board that will meet at least twice a year.[23]

The Leningrad groups have been written about in the official Soviet press (favorably in the central papers Izvestia and Literaturnaya gazeta and negatively in the local paper Leningradskaya pravda [24]. The groups' concern for historical monuments raised the question as to whether they were part of the Pamyat [Memory] movement, which has gained a reputation for being anti-Western and anti-Semitic, with a neo-Slavophile or Russian nationalist agenda. Apparently the Leningrad groups have not been extremely nationalistic or anti-Semitic in their statements, since their treatment by the central Moscow press is favorable; these same newspapers have attacked Pamyat's extremism.

The ecology and cultural groups, along with the literary

164

group Club 1981 (see above under "Discussion Clubs") staged a demonstration in Leningrad against the impending demolition of the Hotel Angleterre, where Russian poet Sergei Yesenin committed suicide in 1925. Leningrad and regional party officials received the groups and heard their protest. Kovalyov signed an article protesting the Angleterre's razing, along with leading Leningrad academician Dmitry Likhachev.

It is not yet known how much such groups will be devoted to questions of nature and environmental protection, and how much to questions of history, culture and the preservation of monuments. Clearly, for the Russians in these groups, "ecology" and the "environment" are concepts not limited to nature and the earth, but to man's own artifacts and the society and culture he creates around him.

Unlike Eastern Europe, it seems that in the Soviet Union, environmental or "green" sentiment at times allies with conservative, anti-Western, tendencies: preserving pre-Soviet Russian history and monuments and preserving nature are part and parcel of resisting the destruction of past and present through "socialist progress" -- the giant construction projects and the "building of communism." Many West European Greens, who are identified with leftist and radical tendencies, may be surprised to find, for example, that a conservative figure like exiled Russian writer Alexander Solzhenitsyn has written critically of the use of nuclear power in the interests of defending not only Mother Nature but Mother Russia.

A report on Valentin Rasputin in Izvestiya in March 1987 dealt with the well-known writer's attitudes towards *glasnost* and *perestroika*. Rasputin is one of the "Village Writers" identified with Russian nationalist or Slavophile sentiment.

In the coming years, as a result of economic reforms and measures, we will get nearer to meeting the population's requirements. This will take place by means of external progress in accordance with the laws of advantageous economics and correct relations between people and the state. But does that mean that external progress will lead to a corresponding progress in our souls? By no means. In a healthy body there does not always dwell a healthy spirit.

Rasputin argued in favor of sound moral values and the avoidance of breeding "cold, business-minded, calculating people on the Western model." He spoke of the pollution of Lake Baykal and Selenga River and commented on *glasnost*:

Glasnost is not just the provision of objective information on the present state of affairs in the country. It is also the need to tell the truth about the past, not omitting to say how, through whose fault it was possible that ruinous arbitrary decisions were taken. Otherwise we will soon be back where we started. It will happen in accordance with the law of suppression and connivance. Total license will breed more total license. The sense of impunity will spread and gradually take over the space that we have cleaned up....Siberia is vast, but greedy hands of ministries and departments, mindful only of their present gain, are longer and they reach to its furthest corners. So far nothing has changed this method of management. [25]

The River Diversion Protest

One of the most striking indications of autonomous protest in the Soviet Union in recent years has been the impressive movement that has gathered to cancel a proposed diversion of northern Siberian rivers into Central Asia and Kazakhstan. The movement was an early harbinger of the *glasnost* campaign in 1986, and recently has been cited frequently and enthusiastically by Soviet officials as proof that public opinion is gaining real power in the Soviet Union and is making its voice heard. Perhaps the movement is not so much an example of tolerance of a genuine grass-roots ecology movement as it is the result of the free expression that emerges during bureaucratic in-fighting, when some forces gain a hearing in the official press and public outspokenness is encouraged. The movement can be seen as an example of a "from the middle" movement among bureaucrats and the elite, rather than the "from below" efforts of ordinary citizens or local communities. But that is all the more reason why top authorities have been compelled to heed it. Writers, engineers, think-tank specialists and government officials in various institutions were actually able to form a lobby of disparate social forces and publicize their cause in the official press (this is in itself a feat under Soviet circumstances), and, what is most surprising, succeed in calling off the officially-sponsored project. The institutions involved in the anti-diversion lobby were the Fifth Section of the USSR Academy of Sciences, a Temporary Scientific-Technical Commission on Problems of Increasing Irrigation headed by Academician A. Yanshin, the All-

Union Geographic Society, the All-Russian Society for the Preservation of Historical and Cultural Monuments, and the USSR Union of Writers. (Among the most outspoken of the writers were the poet Yevgeny Yevtushenko, Village Writer Vladimir Rasputin and Sergei Zalygin, the editor of Novy mir. Among the scientists was Academician Dmitry Likhachev.)

Sergei Voronitsyn, a Russian emigre and researcher for Radio Liberty, has reported regularly on the efforts of the lobby and the recent threat of reversal of their successes.[26] Although the Politburo voted to cancel the project to divert part of the flow of northern and Siberian rivers southwards to the parched areas of Uzbekistan and Kazakhstan, the issue was too large and too many vested interests were at play for a decision from on high to be implemented without opposition. For one, the volume of water involved was to be twenty-five cubic kilometers annually by the year 2000, and was sure to have an impact difficult to control, as bitter experience from the classic Soviet addiction to gigantism has shown. The damage could come in flooding lands and forcing the demise of small villages, but, more ominously, in possibly destroying the biological balance of the Arctic Ocean, and even, as some feared, causing the polar ice caps to melt and upsetting the earth's gravitational forces.

But the "water lobby," or supporters of the project, dismissed these concerns as uninformed alarmism and cited the need of the water-starved Central Asian republics for water (particularly given the demographic fact that the population would be doubling by the turn of the century), for the creation of jobs and the prosperity of the Soviet Union: each cubic kilometer of diverted water was to provide 500 million rubles in new revenues and 50,000 jobs, plus millions of acres of fertile

168

lands.

Another side-effect of the project that was not an argument used by either lobby was the influx of masses of Russians into Central Asia -- the kind of Russification by in-migration that accompanies all giant Soviet construction projects and which would hence not provide local jobs.

And as Sergei Zalygin pointed out in Novy mir,[26] there are some 160 research institutes attached to the Ministry of Land Reclamation and Water Resources, while the number of planners alone is 68,000. This means that it will be an uphill battle to stop the inertia of the bureaucracy and its attempts to keep itself supplied with projects, even at the cost of damaging the environment.

There is evidence that the "water lobby" is now playing the ecology card by citing the drying out of the Aral Sea, which could be saved if the Siberian waters were diverted to it. The issue is far from resolved, as recent publications indicate. Zvezda Vostoka, the Russian-language literary journal of Uzbekistan, apparently broke a two-year press blackout on the subject by publishing a short lead article entitled "Does Central Asia Need Siberian Water?" (No. 6, 1987).[27] The article was accompanied by two letters from specialists in management of water resources to Sergei Zalygin. The proponents of the plan point out that without water, the standard of living of the Central Asian republics, already 30-40 percent below the national average, would drop further. They chastized the anti-diversionists for "touching concern about preserving northern nature" without a "single word of concern about the existing lag in the social and economic development of the Central Asian republics behind the all-Union level and the still more serious

169

picture in prospect."

The diversion battle provides another insight into the tendencies within the mass environmental movement in the Soviet Union: in addition to tending at times to the preservationist and Russian nationalist sentiments of the Village Writers and others, it bears a marked lack of concern for part of the "Third World" within the Soviet empire -- the Central Asian, predominantly Moslem republics. The story of the diversion debate is not merely one of nature-lovers and conservationists versus progress-oriented industrialists and bureaucrats with an eye for windfall profits. It brings into conflict Russians and Asians over centrally-directed planning that benefits the European part of the Soviet Union and the nation as a whole, at the expense of non-Russian local and republican development.

Proposals to form a USSR State Committee for Environmental Protection have been made in recent years and have been viewed with skepticism, since it was unclear how it could remain free from departmental and governmental interests. Sergei Zalygin has proposed that an "anti-project" group be set up to conduct scientific investigations into all the arguments against a project.

In the Baltic republics, environmental awareness is very high, and there are large memberships in officially-controlled nature societies. These societies are typical of the organizations ultimately controlled by the Communist Party bureaucracy, but which have a way of taking on a life of their own even within official strictures, as membership booms and increased opportunities for free expression have been made possible with the *glasnost* campaign.

In Estonia, public awareness of ecological issues is very high.

170

One sociological survey conducted in Estonia two years ago found that:

> 80 percent of the population was "very worried" about the environment. In addition, the cultural elite has become increasingly vocal on environmental issues, and even otherwise relatively obsequious followers of the party line have called for greater local control, especially of the planned excavation of phosphorite. The state of the environment has also been a regular grievance in Estonian samizdat publications; but after a year-long absence of critical material in the Estonian press (which a samizdat document claimed was the result of newly imposed censorship rules on ecological questions), journalists have begun publishing articles on the environment in the official press that are even harsher in tone than those that appeared in samizdat form before. While there has been no indication of a grass-roots "greens" movement, the presence (and political power) of such a group in neighboring Finland has probably not been lost on Finnish television's audience in Northern Estonia.[28]

In March 1986, a group of Estonian scientists issued an open letter protesting Soviet plans to build a large oil harbor at Muuga, near Tallinn, expressing fears of water pollution and a great influx of Russian workers that would further dilute the Estonian population and Russify the character of small Estonian towns. The scientists complained that there had been censorship

171

of the environmental crisis, despite the vaunted *glasnost* campaign in the press.

o   In April 1987, TASS announced that planning work on an underground mine of Europe's largest phosphorite deposit in Estonia had been halted. Bruno Saul, chairman of the Estonian Council of Ministers, stated that if specialists decided that it would cause environmental pollution, the republic would retain the right of veto, and that the interests of economic efficiency would not prevail over the requirements of environmental protection.

In Latvia, more than 400,000 people have joined the Society for the Preservation of Nature and Monuments. The cultural weekly <u>Literatura un Maksla</u> has at times dealt with environmental problems. After it was chastised by the Communist Party leadership for its open discussion, its editor, Janis Skapars, resigned. However, the new editor, Andris Sprogis, has continued to deal with the subject of man's relationship to na ure. [29]

The Lithuanian Preservation of Nature Society has grown from 20,000 members in 1971 to half a million in 1986, and has organized 36 People's Universities offering courses on the environment for over 40,000 students, as well as public lectures.[30]

[1] The original Russian name of this committee is <u>Sovyetsky Komitet zashchity mira</u>, literally Soviet Committee for the Defense of Peace. The name is commonly translated Soviet Peace Committee, and "Soviet Peace Committee" appears on the Committee's own English-language stationery and publications. But we have chosen to retain the literal name to convey the sense in which such official peace committees are concerned with defense as well as peace -- a notion that is lost when the word "defense" is dropped from the translation.

[2] The word *glasnost* has commonly been translated as "openness," but this is misleading; there are other Russian words for the word "openness" like *otkrovyennost*. By giving *glasnost* the connotation of "openness," Westerners misperceive Gorbachev's campaign as creating an open society with the checks and balances of the democratic Western societies. While *glasnost* is a step in the direction of an open society, the Soviet Union remains a one-party system without the pluralism of institutions that make up an open society. *Glasnost*, which comes from the Russian root *glas*, or voice, is better translated as "voicing," "public airing," "public disclosure," i.e., in the sense of uncovering things that were hidden -- which indeed, has been a strength of the *glasnost* campaign. Those who translate the word *glasnost* as "publicity" rather than "publicizing" are erring in the other direction by evoking the manipulative connotations of a Madison Avenue-style public relations campaign. *Glasnost* means publicity, not in the sense of hype, but in the sense of publicizing or exposing. Although the Soviet government

undoubtedly engages in public relations campaigns, and showcases the revelations of *glasnost* in such campaigns, *glasnost* is mainly an effort to deal with domestic ills, not a cynical "active measure" to influence Western public opinion. It is important to note that the word *glasnost* first gained prominence when Dr. Andrei Sakharov used it in his writings in the 1960s, and when the Soviet civil rights activists used it throughout the 1970s with respect to human rights abuse -- which they said required *glasnost*, or publicizing, or exposing. Nowadays, some dissidents are using another word based on the same root, *oglaska*, which also means publicizing, to distinguish their efforts from the government's *glasnost* campaign, which, in their view, often does not go far enough.

[3] Los Angeles Times, "Gorbachev Ally Says Exporting of Revolution is Outdated," July 11, 1987.

[4] From an appeal by nine Soviet refusenik scientists to the Vienna CSCE talks, dated April 20, 1987, published in Samizdat Bulletin, May 1987.

[5] The New York Times, February 12, 1987.

[6] "Statement on Receiving 'Golden Minute' Award From Catalonian Editors and Publishers, Glasnost, no. 1, a samizdat publication published originally in Moscow. The first issue was translated into English by the Center for Democracy in New York in July 1987.

[7] Shatravka's court documents were published in English in

<u>Return Address Moscow</u>, a short-lived magazine of Trust Group activists abroad, vol. 2, in 1983. They were also excerpted in E.P. Thompson's <u>Double Exposure</u>, Merlin Press, London, 1985.

[8] See for example E.P. Thompson, <u>Double Exposure</u>, Merlin Press, London, 1985.

[9] In May 1986, at the annual convention of the International Physicians for the Prevention of Nuclear War, in Cologne, West Germany, Soviet IPPNW representative Dr. Yevgeny Chazov unexpectedly announced that in response to concern from Western peace activists, he had interceded at the Supreme Soviet on behalf of two prisoners from the Moscow Trust Group, Brodsky and Aleksandr Shatravka. Shatravka was first transferred to a psychiatric hospital, then released from labor camp in June and departed from the Soviet Union in July 1986. At first Brodsky's conditions worsened as he was transferred to hard labor, then sentenced to 15 days in a punishment cell while in poor health. But then he was released from labor camp and permitted to emigrate to the West in September 1986.

[10] Martin Walker, <u>The Guardian</u>, April 27, 1987.

[11] Those members who emigrated are Mikhail and Ludmilla Ostrovsky, Lyubov Potekhina, Sergei Batovrin, Valery Godyak, Mark Reitman, Lev Dudkin, Aleksei and Olga Lusnikova, Vitaly Barbash, Lyuba and Pavel Timonin, Aleksandr Shatravka, Yury and Olga Medvedkov, Mariya and Vladimir Fleyshgakker, Gutman Levitan, Vladimir Glezer, Aleksei and Anna Korostylyov, Venyamin Puzankov. (Others associated with the

group, such as Vladmir Lembersky of Moscow and the Gorky activists Alexander Zilber and Marina Zvonova, were also permitted to emigrate.)

[12] Some of the larger section of the Trust Group suspected that the smaller faction had fallen prey to KGB manipulation, a common contention that is difficult to prove among unofficial groups in the strained atmosphere of KGB persecution. But the allegation was strengthened when one factionalist, Olga Sternik, who had been most vocal about disbanding the Group, later turned up at the END Convention in Coventry, England, in July 1987, purporting to represent the Trust Group. The real Trust Group in Moscow, whose candidate for END had been rejected by authorities and was denied permission to travel, exposed the false representation.

[13] For a further discussion of the relation between emigration and the independent peace movement in the USSR, see an essay by Cathy Fitzpatrick entitled "Answering the Hard Questions," and a reply by A. Myasnikov published in the Moscow Trust Group's journal Den' za dnyom [Day By Day], no. 6, June 1987, available from Helsinki Watch.

[14] Irina Krivova, "Historic Moment or Disappointment?", available from Helsinki Watch in a set of documents translated from the Trust Group's magazine Day By Day and released in July 1987.

[15] Translations of the Trust Group's documents concerning the efforts to go to the END Convention were published in a booklet by Helsinki Watch in July 1987.

16 Radio Liberty Research Bulletin, June 10, 1987, no. 23(3436).

17 Kathleen Hendrix, "U.S. Soviet Peace Marchers Take Bold Step in Moscow," Los Angeles Times, July 9, 1987. For an account from the perspective of the Moscow Trust Group, see Den' za dnyom [Day by Day], no. 6, June 1987, and no. 7, July 1987.

18 Sally Laird, "Soviet Literature: What Has Changed?", Index on Censorship, July-August 1987, vol. 16, no. 7.

19 Nikolai Khramov, Is It Easy to Be Truthful?", essay published in samizdat in summer 1987.

20 "Report from Gogolevsky Boulevard," Den' za dnem [Day by Day], no. 5, May 1987. Parts of the journal were excerpted in an English-language booklet published by Helsinki Watch in July 1987.

21 Bill Keller, "Russia's Restless Youth," The New York Times Magazine, July 26, 1987.

22 USSR News Brief, No. 10, May 31, 1987, item 13.

23 USSR News Brief, No. 13, July 15, 1987, item 29.

24 Vera Tolz, "Informal Groups in the USSR," June 11, 1987, Radio Liberty Research, 220/87.

[25] Interview with Valentin Rasputin by TASS correspondent V. Khodiy, "Order in the Soul, Order in the Fatherland," _Izvestiya_, March 15, 1987, from Foreign Broadcast Information Service.

[26] Sergei Voronytsin, "Renewed Debate over Cancelled River Diversion Project, May 27, 1987, RL 205/87, _Radio Liberty Research_ no. 22(3435).

[27] Ann Sheehy, "The Central Asian Siberian River Diversion Lobby Hits Back, RL 243/87, June 29, 1987, _Radio Liberty Research_, no. 27 (3440). Sheehy quotes _Zvezda Vostoka_, no. 6, 1987.

[28] Toomas Ilves, Radio Free Europe _Research_, March 20, 1987, RAD Background Report/42.

[29] Dzintra Bungs, RAD Background Report/42, 20 March 1987, Radio Free Europe _Research_.

[30] Saulius Girnius, "The Environment and Eastern Europe: Lithuania," RAD Background Report/42, March 20, 1987.

VI. YUGOSLAVIA

There is peace if freedom is guaranteed by law and if such laws are, or can be, made use of. Peace is a concept which is defined by a society which is independent of the state, contrary to the state and distinct from it. Society in this sense is preliminarily called a civil society. Peace is a concept of a civil society. -- Ljubljana Peace Group, address to Western peace movement, July 1986.

Since Tito broke with Stalin and was expelled from the Cominform in 1948, Yugoslavia has represented the hope of a more humane and democratic path to communism for many in the West. Despite much evidence to the contrary, Yugoslavia's system of self-management is cited as the way in which non-Soviet socialism could work. Yugoslavia is not a member of the Warsaw Pact, and is a leader among the neutral and non-aligned countries. It is heavily subsidized by the U.S. government, among other Western countries, which see it as a bulwark against the Soviet Union. Yet its Communist regime can be as repressive as other East European nations. Although there is sausage in the stores and photocopying shops open to the public in downtown Belgrade, there are approximately 1,300 political prisoners in Yugoslavia, more than in Czechoslovakia, Hungary and Poland combined.

Yugoslavia is beset by conflicts among its six distinct republics and two autonomous regions and a struggle is being waged between liberals and hardliners in the country's collective leadership, with differences defined along republic lines, ranging from Western-leaning Slovenia to repressive Bosnia-Herzogovina.

179

There is a mixture of increased press freedom and civil rights activity, with more book bannings and newspaper closings reported in recent years.

In 1984, police raided a meeting of a loose network of students and professors called the "free university" on a night that veteran dissident Milovan Djilas was speaking. Dozens of people were arrested and hundreds interrogated, and one activist died under mysterious circumstances after questioning in police custody. Finally, six Belgrade scholars were subjected to a well-publicized show trial, the first since Tito's death in 1980, and the regime unsuccessfully attempted to justify its charges of conspiracy. After international protest, notably from the West German Green Party, four defendants were acquitted and two handed relatively light sentences. To date, only one, Miodrag Milic, has been forced to report to jail to serve his term. But the "free university" did not resume after the trial, and free speech trials have continued since the Scholars' Trial, mainly outside Belgrade. Despite a civil rights activists' vigorous campaign against Article 133 ("hostile propaganda"), there is no real indication that such trials will cease in the near future. Although the majority of political prisoners were arrested for nationalist activity, according to the state prosecutors' reports published in the official press, two-thirds of the political prisoners were arrested for "verbal crimes" (free speech) under Art. 133 -- not for the violent crimes that Westerners may associate with separatist movements.

The autonomous province of Kosovo, where the majority of the population is ethnic Albanian, is the site of unrest and separatist demonstrations that led to a de facto state of martial law several years ago. Trials of hundreds of adults and high

school students continue. Many teenagers are serving heavy
sentences for leafletting or writing graffiti.

Ljubljana

A decade ago, an independent youth culture surfaced in
Ljubljana and was eventually repressed by the authorities. But
from these origins, independent peace and ecology groups
emerged and became increasingly emboldened. Known as the
Ljubljana Peace Group, they were launched under the aegis of
the Socialist Youth Alliance of Yugoslavia. They began to stage
demonstrations and issue publications, such as the following:

o   On Victory Day, May 9, 1985, about 200 members
    and supporters of the Ljubljana Peace Group (many
    reports said there were many more participants) staged a
    procession through the city in protest against the military
    parade held that day in Belgrade. Police did not attempt
    to stop the procession.

o   On April 17, 1986, the Ljubljana Peace Group
    distributed about 150 leaflets on the street on a day when
    meetings to protest the U.S. attack on Libya were
    organized by the Socialist Youth Federation elsewhere in
    Yugoslavia. The Ljubljana activists condemned the attack
    on Libya, but also called for the withdrawal of Soviet
    ships from the area. The leaflet was written in the form
    of a letter to the embassies of the United States and
    Libya and to the Presidency of Yugoslavia. The appeal
    also called for Yugoslavia and other countries to end
    participation in the arms trade and to close military

181

schools for training Libyan military forces. A protest meeting organized by the Ljubljana Peace Group was attended by approximately 3,000 people in Maribor. The meeting sent a letter to the U.S., the USSR and Libya, as well as to the Yugoslav Secretary of Foreign Affairs.

It is natural that such alternative, independent movements would arise in Slovenia, the most liberal and Western-oriented of the Yugoslav republics. What can be published openly in the officially-recognized Slovenian press, for example, can be grounds for prosecution in neighboring Croatia, as was proved this year with the trial of Dobroslav Paraga, a student and ex-political prisoner sentenced for exposing deplorable prison conditions in Croatia in the Slovenian press.

The movement is coordinated by two groups, the Peace Movement Working Group at the Republic Conference of the Socialist Youth Alliance and the People for Peace Culture of the Student Cultural Center, which produce an information bulletin, Peace Movement in Yugoslavia. The movements devote their attention mainly to issues of domestic militarism, advocating alternative service for conscientious objectors, voicing opposition to the proposed introduction of military service for women, urging a ban on war toys, and so on, similar to the movements in East Germany, Hungary, Poland and the Soviet Union. Since Yugoslav travel policies are relatively lenient, activists have been able to attend international peace conferences, like the END convention in Europe, and have established contacts with a number of Eastern and Western groups. In October 1987, the Ljublana peace activists plan to host an international conference of their own for a network of independent East-West peace

182

activists.

Although Slovenia is relatively liberal, it is not completely free of political oppression. Sociologist Tomas Mastnak, fellow of the Institute for Marxist Studies of the Slovenian Academy of Arts and Sciences and a spokesperson for the Ljubljana Peace Group, was charged with "denigrating leaders of another socialist republic" for criticizing the manner in which hardliner Branko Mikulic, the new head of the government, was chosen. He made his remarks over Radio Student in January 1986, and the youth newspaper Mladina was due to print them the following day. But authorities intervened to ban the newspaper and opened up a case against Mastnak with the public prosecutor. After a flood of domestic protest from a variety of communist and independent organizations, as well as Western peace and human rights groups, the charges were dropped.

In July 1986, the Ljubljana Peace Group issued an address to the Western peace movement, outlining its positions on the division of Europe and the East-West dialogue. It has remained eager to receive responses from Western peace groups.[1] The statement echoes many similar documents from the other East European peace movements, and concludes:

> There is...peace if citizens are obedient to state authority and if the state authorities suppress the citizens. There is said to be peace in Poland...[and] Czechoslovakia. State dictatorship over society, guaranteed by the national or some other fraternal army, is peace. There is peace if such a dictatorship is recognized as far as the internal affair of the state concerned, and if nobody interferes in these internal

affairs. Such peace...represents a concept that is defined by the state.

Nevertheless, peace cannot be a state concept only. If we are able and willing to listen, we can hear more and more people saying that there is a fundamental link between peace and the assurance of and respect for human and civil rights, a decent life for individuals and an independent social life, with freedom and democracy. There is peace if freedom is guaranteed by law and if such laws are or can be made use of. Peace is a concept which is defined by a society which is independent of the state, contrary to the state and distinct from it. Society in this sense is preliminarily called a civil society. Peace is a concept of a civil society.

The Ljubljana Peace Group defined itself in the document as an independent peace movement:

> a social movement, separate and distinct in its principles from state peace policy. The Peace Movement is therefore independent by definition: independent of state organizations and structures, and, at the same time, on principle independent of state boundaries. The only boundary that is common to the state and civil society is the one that divides them. This is more true the further society is emancipated from the state....Civil-social peace can be considered to be the demolition of the boundaries between civil societies; it can be considered to be the process of the

internationalization of the civil society.

In an interview with East European Reporter,[2] Mastnak cautions Westerners not to apply the East European framework to the Yugoslav case, given the differences in their histories, their unique geopolitical position between East and West, and their multi-national structure, unique in Central-Eastern Europe. Mastnak is able to explain succinctly the riddle of how Yugoslavia, after breaking with Stalinism and making overtures to the West, could remain a repressive society. In his analysis of Yugoslavia's special features, it becomes evident that an independent peace and environmental movement may be the only type of movement that could cross the boundaries of Yugoslavia's disparate republics and at the same time create ties with the Western social movements.

Authoritarianism in Yugoslavia comes in strange and surprising forms. While there are strong decentralizing trends, these have nothing to do with democracy or pluralism. There is no necessary correlation between decentralization and democracy. In our system, decentralized power structures coexist with authoritarianism, which is often strongest at the local level, for instance at the grass roots levels of civil society....We should not try to repeat what Solidarity tried -- and failed -- to do. We should try to invent new forms of democratic activity appropriate to our particular situation....Inventing the single issue-oriented political campaigns common in Western European democracies would be a very good start...we lack a democratic tradition and popularly shared memories of a strong and independent civil society. Issue-oriented campaigns -- involving women, opponents of nuclear power, gays, pacifists and others -- are crucial for filling this gap, and for producing a democratic culture in Yugoslavia.

Anti-Nuclear Power Movement

The largest public reponse to the Chernobyl accident in Eastern Europe came from the protests and petitions in Yugoslavia. The Yugoslav populace was not warned about the dangers of the radioactive cloud until more than a week after the accident on May 3, the day after the cloud had already drifted over the country. Several days later, after radio and television reports from Austria and Italy were received, the press began to recommend safety measures. But like many other things in Yugoslavia, the advice varied in each of the country's six republics:

> In some, officials asserted there was no danger; in others, they exhorted the people to take extreme precautions. Apparently the great nuclear cloud from Chernobyl had subdivided into six smaller clouds, with degrees of radioactivity ranging from benign to lethal. [3]

But the public was still in a better position to make their fears heard than in neighboring Soviet bloc states. After Chernobyl, a public opinion poll showed that 75 percent of

Yugoslavs oppose nuclear power and only 2 percent consider it safe, despite the efforts of a "nuclear lobby" of scientists and bureaucrats who make an economic and technological argument for relying on nuclear power. Although the government's discussion of the plants receded from the public scene after Chernobyl, it was feared that it would easily be revived after a cold winter with electricity shortages.[4]

The "nuclear lobby" is believed to take advantage of the fact that in a Communist society where the flow of information is suppressed in general, it can easily gain access to the government without public scrutiny. Dejan Dimov, higher counselor in the Yugoslav Chamber of Commerce, stated in 1985 that the nuclear lobby was stronger and worked more efficiently than in the West:

> Our political system is being misused in the present situation, so that individual anonymous, but very powerful groups, political and scientific in nature, not only manipulate, but also exert full control over information which, as a rule, I don't know why, is strictly confidential, so that one cannot discuss it. [5]

In June 1986, the first congress of the Yugoslav anti-nuclear movement was held in Belgrade, attended by ecological and peace groups. Vukasin Pavlovic, a leader of the movement, said "We are not an opposition; we want to work through existing institutions." Even so, officials reacted by making the usual accusation that the protest was nevertheless political and even alien and subversive -- imported from the West.

The largest signature campaign against nuclear power in Eastern Europe -- and one of the largest in Eastern Europe for any cause -- was unexpectedly launched by high-school students in Belgrade, Serbia, even <u>before</u> the accident at Chernobyl on April 26, 1986.

Anti-nuclear power protest has been around for a while in Yugoslavia. In 1979, for example, residents of the Dalmation island of Vir voted against the construction of a nuclear plant, fearing its harmful effects on the environment.[6] When news about offers for the construction of four nuclear power plants first appeared in Yugoslavia in 1986, war veterans from Bosanska Krajina were the first to protest, followed by 132 employees of the Belgrade factory Electro-Istok. About 3,000 students of Novi Sad University also generated a petition. But the Mosa Pijade Belgrade Secondary School broke the record for all petitioning in Yugoslavia when they collected 70,000 signatures. (As far as is known, the only other petitions in Eastern Europe that have garnered many thousands more signatories were for religious freedom by Catholics in Lithuania; a demand to stop the Danube hydroelectric project in Hungary gathered an impressive 10,000.)

According to an article on April 13, 1986, by Dragan Jovanovic in <u>Nin</u>, the official Belgrade daily, Aleksandr Knezevic, a student at Mosa Pijade, was inspired to start the petition campaign when he read in the press about the plans to start construction of the nuclear plants. Knezevic went to Krstimir Simic, his high-school headmaster, and obtained an agreement to continue the action with the support of the Municipal Conference (i.e., Board) of the Federation of Youth of Stari Grad (a municipality in Belgrade), which backed the petition after a meeting in March. The response was so enthusiastic that some people wanted to organize a protest march, but this idea was rejected. But it was agreed by the Municipal

188

Conference that all the schools in Stari Grad would give financial assistance to cover the cost of distributing the petition in the schools. However, when the Conference's president was replaced, the new official did not want to take up the controversial cause, particularly at the start of his term. Suddenly, support dried up and the official who had printed the students' petition and had been the first to receive them suddenly disavowed any connection to the issue. Some schools began inquiring with the Secretary of the Interior to see if the petition had really been approved by higher-ups. Knezevic was told that the signatures to date would be burned before a commission. In repeated telephone calls at night, he was threatened that he would be sentenced to 60 days in jail and that his parents would be fired from their jobs. But he survived to tell the story on a Yugoslav television program and considered the harassment to be "normal" for an action that involved so many thousands of people.

After meeting with the student initiators of the campaign, Headmaster Simic was summoned to the Municipal Committee of the League of Communists, along with all the headmasters and party secretaries of all the secondary schools of the Stari Grad municipality. It was decided that a petition would not be printed, but the letter by the Mosa Pijade students could be read at classes throughout the republic of Serbia and each class could declare itself in favor or against the issue. Simic said that far more than 70,000 signatures could have been garnered if the Party Committee had not essentially stopped the campaign with the decision at this meeting not to move the petition through existing official channels.

A photocopied letter was sent around to the schools; of 464

in Serbia, 110 responded. No schools from Kosovo replied, but letters came from Danilovgrad, Teslic and Zagreb in Croatia. The letter provoked a response from the pro-nuclear movement as well. A group of assistant professors and undergraduates from the Machine-Building Faculty, which is involved with nuclear technology, invited themselves to Mosa Pijade School to "educate" the anti-nuclear petitioners.

Officials were uneasy about the youth initiative. When asked by the Nin correspondent about the official attitude towards organized youth initiatives, Zoran Andjelkovic, President of the Republic Conference of the Federation of Youth of Serbia, explained:

> Young people are increasingly turning to "individual political actions" when motivated by their interest. The so-called alternative content in music, the graffiti, the petitions, are part of a new youth vocation....Such "informal" and "non-institutional" political expressions by young people have so far mainly been opposed. The Federation of Youth sometimes has a narrow approach to organizational issues.

Although apparently sympathetic, Andjelkovic himself volunteered the opinion that the "70,000 voices so expressed are not the best way to express the political and social subjectivity of the young generation." Clearly, this "subjectivity" had to be voiced through "objective" state youth organizations in order to be legitimate.

The Yugoslav press has generally given a fair amount of

space to the nuclear power issue, both pro and con, reflecting the efforts of Yugoslavia's "nuclear power lobby" as well as grass-roots initiatives to stop the construction of the power stations. Yugoslavia is the only East European nation where protests after Chernobyl have been continuously massive and have led to at least a postponement of the construction of nuclear plants. The Socialist Youth Alliance in Ljubljana condemned the Soviet's handling of the disaster and called for an end to nuclear power. The Ljubljana Peace Group issued a strongly-worded statement on Chernobyl demanding complete information, punishment of those responsible for delays in information, claim of compensation from the Soviet Union, a moratorium on nuclear plants, a referendum on the construction of the planned Prevlaka plant, and the formation of independent nuclear energy agencies. About 2,000 people took part in a demonstration where the declaration was read. The Yugoslav press, which is more open than the Soviet bloc media, has carried frank criticism of past nuclear policies and expressed alarm about the serious consequences of nuclear energy for the country's future.

On May 10, 1987, more than a year after the Chernobyl accident, Mladost, the bi-monthly organ of the Federation of Socialist Youth of Yugoslavia, ran an article entitled "Nuclear Power Plants - Stop!" calling for a moratorium on the building of atomic energy plants. The Congress of the Federation of the Socialist Youth of Yugoslavia adopted an anti-nuclear resolution at its most recent Congress, following the examples of the young people in the Socialist Youth Alliance in Slovenia, who were the first to bring such autonomous protest into the official socialist organizations to help strengthen and legitimize them.

As urgent as the environmental concern was the economic

impact for Yugoslavia. While Yugoslavs feared that their poor, foreign-indebted country would be a natural magnet for wealthier nations' inferior and perhaps unsafe nuclear technology as well as radioactive waste, they also saw that the immediate effect of the construction would be to push Yugoslavia further into debt: Mladost claimed that the building of only one atomic plant by the year 2000 would incur a $10 billion debt. Moreover, as Mladost pointed out, there was the temptation to turn peaceful nuclear energy programs into military ones that could significantly alter the country's purported non-aligned status.

In the fall of 1986, some Belgrade intellectuals formed a Committee for the Protection of Man and the Environment with Biljana Jovanovic as president. Ms. Jovanovic is a member of the Serbian Writers' Union. Svetlana Slapsak, a member of the Committee, is President of the Committee for Freedom of Artistic Expression in the Serbian Writers' Union. Her husband, a Slovenian who lives in Ljubljana, is also active in the environmental movement. The Committee's environmental activity concentrates on writing petitions and publicizing issues by preparing articles for publication in Knijevna rec, the book review that is the organ of the Serbian Writers' Union, and in the Slovenian newspapers Mladina and Tribuna. The articles deal with air and water pollution in various industrial centers in Yugoslavia and with the nuclear power issue. One of the Committee's publications spoke of the failure of the government to continue regular announcements about the level of radioactivity in Yugoslavia after the Chernobyl accident. Immediately after the explosion, an ad hoc emergency Radiation Committee was set up within the Yugoslav Federal Assembly and began regularly announcing the level of radiation. But after the new Prime Minister, Branko Mikulic, came to office on May 15, 1987, he put a stop to the announcements. In addition to environmental causes, Svetlana Slapsak has taken up protest about universal compulsory draft without alternative service and the drafting of women into the Yugoslav army and has defended those convicted for non-violent political activity.

In April 1987, the central federal student association, the Socialist Youth League, which is advocating protest against atomic energy, invited Prime Minister Mikulic to speak at their Presidium meeting. Instead, an official of the Ministry of Energy and Industry came to speak to the young people and tried to dismiss their fears about pollution, radiation and increasing the national debt.

Yugoslavia's peace and ecology protest is probably the best example of the way in which independent protest is infused into existing officially-established organizations or agencies, in the process making them less dependent on the state. The existing structures that enable the Communist parties to instantly mobilize millions of people to denounce, say, the latest aggressive imperialist act, can be used for environmental protest once a decision is made by the top bureaucracy to accept the issue as legitimate.

In an article in The Nation (May 9, 1987), a well-known Zagreb feminist, Slavenka Drakulich, author of Mortal Sins of Feminism, wrote on the phenomenon of the transformation of the official Socialist Youth League into a channel for spontaneous youth protest. Although the League is "supposed to transmit Communist Party ideology to quiet and obedient young people, on the Soviet model," it was mainly pro-forma and insignificant, generally seen by youth as "bureaucratic and useless." Government leaders in turn complain about the political apathy of young people, by which they really meant the lack of participation in "mass excitement imposed from above," as Lev Kreft, the former leader of the Socialist Youth League, phrased it:

> Therefore, the recent restructuring of the Slovenian branch of the organization, opening itself to peace, feminist and ecological groups, came as a surprise. The group's actions and methods are even more surprising to the Yugoslav public. It advocates the workers' right to strike, the abolition of capital punishment, a referendum on the construction of nuclear power plants, and the institution of alternative military service. It stages protest marches, makes public demands, circulates petitions, and organizes demonstrations and acts of civil disobedience -- all of which are absolutely new to the Yugoslav scene. (Drakulich)

It is not only that existing structures did not take up the issues that interested youth, there is really no place for them in society. As Drakulich points out:

> ...the economic crisis has made the position of young people even more marginal, politically and otherwise. They constitute the largest percentage of the unemployed and wait an average of two or three years for their first job. The patriarchal mentality as well

194

as a shortage of apartments force them to share their parents' households even after they are married and have children. All important positions in politics and management are held by those who are relatively old as gerontocracy is a well-known state of affairs in all socialist countries.

Given these constrictions, the young people infused the official organizations with their enthusiasm, to "keep the system going but, at the same time, to change it for the better" -- thus by-passing the route of repression and preoccupation with personal defense that became the lot of Yugoslavia's civil rights and nationalist dissidents.

Conscientious Objection

Resistance to compulsory draft has only recently become an issue in Yugoslavia, where the Army's influence is powerful and there is widespread popular support for the army that emerged from the partisan fight for national liberation during World War II. In a country that is supposedly nonaligned and poised between East and West, the question of a home defense is an emotional issue. Pacifism and conscientious objection are not acceptable to official Yugoslav Marxist ideology or to general patriotism, and there is no legal provision for alternative service. Art. 214 of the Federal Criminal Code provides for up to five years of imprisonment for those who go into hiding to avoid conscription. Those who leave the country or remain abroad to avoid the draft may be punished by from one to ten years of imprisonment. In time of war, draft avoidance is punishable by at least five years of imprisonment or death. [7]

According to Slavenka Drakulic, each year about 25 men are jailed for conscientious objection, many of them members of the Jehovah's Witnesses, Nazarenes and others who refuse to bear arms on religious grounds. According to the official Yugoslav news agency TANJUG, in the last 15 years, 152 people have been sentenced for refusing to carry arms because of religious beliefs, mainly Jehovah's Witnesses, Seventh-Day Adventists, and Nazarenes. The following are examples:

o   Ivan Cecko, 30, a Jehovah's Witness from Maribor in Slovenia had already spent seven years in prison as a conscientious objector when he was re-sentenced to five additional years in September 1986. (The military court in Belgrade had sentenced him to four years in 1979 and five years in 1983; [three served]). In November, he was unexpectedly released and the Military High Court held a closed hearing, to which even Cecko himself and his lawyer were not invited. Cecko had originally been tried on three charges; two were dropped at the hearing and only one retained -- not responding to a draft summons, for which the sentence had been 11 months, reduced to 7. He was released from a Belgrade prison and ordered to serve the remaining four months in Maribor. But after arriving home, he reportedly remained free. [8]

o   Zvone Vajs of Gornja Radgona, Slovenia, a Jehovah's Witness, had previously spent 3 years and 6 months in prison under Art. 202 of the Criminal Code (refusal to bear arms) when he was sentenced again on December 23, 1986, under Art. 214 (refusing the draft and avoiding military service), to one year and 6 months. He was free at least up until March while his lawyer was appealing the case.

o   Six Slovenian conscientious objectors from Maribor were sent summonses in October 1986, despite the fact that they had all refused to perform any kind of military service at least once in the past, and had all repeatedly been sentenced to long-term prison sentences. In November, the military conscription office retracted their summonses without explanation, although this was the time when the question of civilian service was being debated by authorities. It seemed as if their cases had been dropped. But in February 1987, all were summoned to report to military units in various places in Yugoslavia in March. The cases are as follows:

Janko Cehtel, born July 25, 1961, served two sentences, total of four years; Rajko Valenta, born August 10, 1961, served two sentences, total of four years; Anton Bergaver, born January 10, 1962, served one sentence, total of three years; Bojan Miglic, born July 28, 1961, served two sentences, total of four years; Ivan Beraver, born April 25, 1965, served one sentence, total of ten months; Peter Jezernik, born January 3, 1962, served one sentence, total of 2-1/2 years.

o   On December 10, 1986, U.N. Human Rights Day, the Ljubljana Peace Group collected signatures for an appeal to the Yugoslav government concerning the issue of conscientious objection, urging the authorities not only to recognize the right in Yugoslavia but to urge that it be recognized as a right by the United Nations. The Group organized a street stall that day and exhibited materials from Amnesty International, Helsinki Watch, the Bertrand Russell Tribunal, and Yugoslav human rights committees, as well as the War Resisters International annual report on prisoners of conscience. In addition, the peace activists collected signatures to petitions in support of political prisoners in Yugoslavia, the Moscow Trust Group, as well as petitions on introducing alternative service, introducing a referendum on nuclear power, abolishing war toys and replacing them with non-violent toys, etc. [9]

The Ljubljana Peace Group took up the defense of Cecko in the hopes of raising a public debate about conscientious objection and to propose that alternative civilian service be made available.[10] The Central Committee of the Communist League of Slovenia supported the proposal for alternative service and opened public discussion in the Socialist League of Working People, a front that purportedly includes all social groups, even clerics. The discussion on conscientious objection soon became a litmus test for the degree of democracy within Yugoslavia as a whole and highlighted the differences and confrontations between the republics. The Slovenians were the only Central Committee among Yugoslavia's republics to take up the issue; the others not only refused to open up a public debate about it, they condemned the idea and its initiators. Apparently, the military was allowed to make the decision to ban the debate. The Secretary of Defense, Adm. Branko Mamula, announced that even discussion of the issue would weaken Yugoslavia's defenses; he did, however, instruct the military courts that defendants should not be sentenced repeatedly for the same offense of refusing the draft.

In December 1986, the All People's Defense and Social Self-Protection Coordinating Council of the Socialist Alliance of Working People of Yugoslavia, a public front organization under control of the Yugoslav Communist Party, unanimously resolved that alternative service was "unacceptable." Col. Gen. Milan Daljevic, President of the Council, vigorously denounced the Ljubljana youth movements, hinting ominously that they were inspired by "internal and external" enemies and that in addition to "ideo-political" work, other unspecified "measures" were to be taken against them.

> ...these movements are increasingly becoming movements for negative politicization and the manipulation of some young people. It is very significant that these movements have started to emerge at the time of an intensified special war against [Yugoslavia] and our system...Judging from the slogans and the aggressiveness of a number of the young supporters of these movements, one begins to feel more and more that they are largely a screen behind which both the external and internal enemy is hiding. This is why I am in favor of undertaking more resolute, organized, and concrete ideopolitical and other measures against the damaging and unacceptable activity of these movements....This should be done soon because many indicators show that this can be a road to a multiparty system. [11]

In January 1987, the Macedonian League of Communists also resolved that alternative service was "unacceptable" and that the autonomous peace movements are "aimed and breaking up and weakening" the Yugoslav Armed Forces and chastized those responsible for ideological indoctrination as slackening in their vigilance. There were the usual calls for "sharpening personal and collective responsibility" in "implementing the law:"

> ...hostile activity...in particular against the Armed Forces [and] attempts at confrontation between a section of the young generation and the policy and system of all-people's defense...have not been sufficiently exposed and condemned by our public...somebody from "above" should raise these questions and take action....It is necessary to ensure a more organized opposition to the theses on the so-called peace trends or various naive understandings of war and the defense of the country. A defeatist defense policy is being put forward in the guise of democratic dialogue. [12]

In January 1987, Borba and others joined the chorus of denunciation of the proposal, revealing in the process the real extent of democracy in Yugoslavia:

> Those behind this initiative very persistently and, in some people's opinion, fairly aggressively insisted that their proposal be discussed on a larger Yugoslav scale. At the same time, they invoked the democratic rules of the game, but failed to see, as was

shown, that the achieved level of the democratization of social relations cannot be measured by how much the public stage is open for setting various ideas and political concepts against each other. Democracy does not only imply permanent openness for the confrontation of various ideas and for new concepts, but also for their democratic selection *in accordance with the fundamental tenets of the Yugoslav League of Communists and our society. The essence of democracy does not really lie in initiating and conducting a general discussion about initiatives which, even at first glance, clearly appear to be unacceptable.* [Emphasis added.] [13]

In its January 1987 newsletter, the Ljubljana peace movement wrote an article on conscientious objection, describing the ramifications of their role. An excerpt of the English-language edition is as follows:

COs are creating a different state of conscience on our planet not only by refusing military service, refusing to pay War taxes and refusing to work in military industrial complexes, but mostly with their presence, with their Life Energy and by manifesting this kind of energy. CO therefore does not only manifest in confronting the state's policy but in the first place it manifests in establishing a whole network of people who are based on different social axioms and communications. Networks like Quakers, pacifists, various kinds of religious and spiritual

201

groups, tax resisters, peace movements, Third World support groups and many others are arising and are starting to communicate with each other East and West, North and South. These networks are made at a level independent from the state, and independent of race, sex and social position. They are based on the principle of receptivity rather than on the principle of resistance. Receptivity in the sense of receptivity to society, and resistance in the sense of resistance to state concepts. [sic]

The Ljubljana peace activists do not only see conscientious objection within the context of their own society, but see the issue as a route to what they call the "internationalization of civil society" and "one of the processes in establishing peaceful coexistence on our planet." They reject the criticism that they are cowards or are weakening the state.

> We also understand COs as persons deeply involved in defending society, when the notion of the security of society is placed in a wider context than the common understanding of security that is identified with the state's defense and military power. We understand security of society to be its social, ecological, economic and human rights securities, which are in many cases threatened by the states themselves.

Meanwhile, the discussion on conscientious objection continues, and Slovenian authorities have agreed to find an alternative to long-term imprisonment of religious believers like the Jehovah's Witnesses, but that alternative will still be a form of military service, not civilian work. This raises the problem of equality of citizens, believers and non-believers alike, before the law and in an especially peculiar way for a Marxist state: why can't atheists also be conscientious objectors?

Although the issue was suppressed from national public debate, the Slovenian initiative at least influenced practices somewhat: in some cases, young men who had already been imprisoned once were not re-summoned by the draft, while in the past, the practice was to summon them and imprison them repeatedly. The possibility of non-combatant service has also been introduced. In short, in Yugoslavia, as in Poland, the tactic will probably continue to be one of accommodating protesters but not fully institutionalizing and legalizing conscientious objection and alternative service.

Zagreb

In Zagreb, the capital of Croatia, a neighbor of Slovenia but where authorities are much more hard-line on the political spectrum and much less tolerant of dissent and independent initiative, a peace and environmental group has also emerged, calling itself Svarun. Formed in 1986 by young people, it was comprised mainly of high-school and university students in Zagreb, within the Socialist Youth Alliance. But a year after it attempted to register with official agencies, it has still not been granted status as an organization. It sees its main task as starting a democratic discussion of peace, environmental, feminist and spiritual matters in Croatia, particularly in the schools. The

Ljubljana Peace Group described Svarun in their January 1987 newsletter:

> While sharing with other groups in Europe and in the world the characteristics of being a non-hierarchical anti-authoritarian group striving for a safe, clean world, Svarun is, in many ways, in a special situation. Unlike our "geographically closest" companions, the Slovenian movements, which have been active for years and have become a power to be reckoned with, we have only just assembled in April 1986 and haven't even been fully registered yet!

One of Svarun's chief concerns is the non-violent raising of children, the abolition of war toys, and the promotion of other, creative toys. They also seek to disseminate a "peace culture" and peace information more broadly to the population so that it reaches them on a personal level. Svarun opposes the Yugoslav nuclear program and demands a nation-wide referendum on the use of nuclear energy.

Yugoslavia -- Notes

[1] This pamphlet is available from Helsinki Watch.

[2] East European Reporter. Vol.2, No. 2., 1986.

[3] Slavenka Drakulich, "Hard Rain Falls on Yugoslavia: No Ecological Independence," The Nation, February 14, 1987.

[4] Ibid.

[5] Dragan Jovanovic, "Nuclear Power Stations in Public," Nin, March 2, 1986.

[6] Milan Andreyevich, "The Environment and Eastern Europe," Radio Free Europe, March 20, 1987, RAD BR/42.

[7] Yugoslavia: Prisoners of Conscience, Amnesty International Publications, p. 57.

[8] Information Booklet: Peace Movement in Yugoslavia, Vol. 3. No. 1, January 1987. Issued in English by Peace Movement Working Group and People for Peace Culture, in Slovenia.

[9] Ibid.

[10] Slavenka Drakulich, "Yugoslav Youth Stirs it Up: The Case of Ivan Cecko," The Nation, May 9, 1987.

[11] "Civilian Military Service Unacceptable," Politika,

December 25, 1986.

[12] TANJUG, January 13, 1987.

[13] Ljubiaka Milosevik, "Everybody is Equal in Defense," TANJUG, <u>Borba</u>, January 8, 1987.

APPENDIX I: THE PRAGUE APPEAL

We hereby make public the Prague Appeal which has been drafted in the form of a letter to this summer's peace movement congress by a group of Charter 77 signatories representing a cross-section of opinion. We are submitting this draft of a joint statement for discussion to the signatories of Charter 77 and all citizens and institutions who are not indifferent to how we will continue to live together on this continent. We will welcome all expressions of agreement or criticism, as well as individual or collective responses to this proposal from abroad, and especially from this, to date, still-divided continent.

We trust that the debate will give rise to suggestions and proposals which will help overcome the obstacles standing in the way of a united, democratic and sovereign Europe of free citizens and nations. Only such a Europe will be capable of acting as an effective partner in the task of establishing peace and tackling the growing crisis of today's world.

Jiri Dienstbier

Eva Kanturkova

Petruska Sustrova

March 11, 1985

Dear Friends:

It is forty years now since there was a war on European soil. Notwithstanding, Europe has not been a continent of peace. Far from it, as Europe has been one of the main points of friction between the two power blocs, tension has been a permanent feature throughout the period, thereby posing a threat to the entire world. Were a war to break out here, it would turn not only into a world conflict, but most likely into one that would prove fatal for the entire planet.

The reason Europe has played this baleful role is the divided state of our continent. Our common hope, therefore, lies in overcoming this division. This can only be achieved through a conscious decision by all to gradually transform the very political realities which are responsible for the present situation.

One reason why the state of non-war has lasted forty years is the fact that both sides have respected the situation created when the spheres of military operations agreed on at Yalta degenerated into military and political blocs. What governs the continued efforts to maintain, defend and strengthen the status quo are fears about destabilization of the balance that has been achieved. For this reason, a process of change will call for great sensitivity. It cannot be accompanied by threats of achieving superiority on either side. On the contrary, it will require guarantees and assurances, as well as an evaluation of the present situation in all its component aspects. It will be essential to acknowledge the present state of affairs as the basis for change to dispel fears of a revival of the old dangers which have led to catastrophe twice in this century already. However, the chances of moving beyond the present situation are not altogether as unfavorable as they might seem.

The Conference on Security and Cooperation in Europe and its Final Act signed in Helsinki, are, like the subsequent talks and the Final Document of Madrid, not just an acknowledgment of the status quo, but also constitute a program of European and Euro-American cooperation. Throughout this process, the negotiations have not been conducted between the blocs but between equal partners, a fact which has underlined the independence of all participating states and established in principle the sort of relations which, if implemented, would open the way to the unification of Europe. Furthermore, the principle of the indivisibility of peace, a legacy of European culture, has been embodied in relations not only between states, but also between the state and society, and between citizens and governments.

The requirement that governments should fulfill all their undertakings and obligations has not been made full use of by the peace movement. Such binding agreements sanctioned by international law constitute a framework whereby citizens may not only exercise public oversight of governments but also find imaginative ways of loosening ossified positions. Because of the great variety of conditions in the different countries, there has been a tendency to stress the dissimilarities. However, these must be fully grasped and respected if a common approach and European solidarity are to be achieved.

A democratic and sovereign Europe is inconceivable so long as individual citizens, groups of citizens or nations are denied the right to take part in decisions affecting not only their everyday lives, but also their very survival. Within a framework of cooperation and dialogue among all those who genuinely seek to overcome the present dangerous situation, it should be possible to come forward with different disarmament initiatives and proposals: the creation of nuclear-free and neutral zones, the encouragement of relations between individuals, groups and states, support for agreements on non-aggression, as well as the renunciation of the use of force or nuclear weapons and, finally, regional treaties of all kinds, including, for example, rapprochement between the EEC and the CMEA. Within this framework, citizens would be able to campaign against the insensitive treatment of the environment and, taking governments at their word, analyze government policies and their likely effects. In short, it is necessary to support all actions by individuals, groups and governments seeking the rapprochement and free association of European nations while rejecting any measures which might postpone or thwart the achievement of this ideal.

In our pursuit of these aims we can no longer avoid those issues which have so far been taboo, one of which is the division of Germany.

If our aim is European unification, then no one can be denied the right to self-determination; and this applies equally to the Germans. As with all other rights, though, this must not be enforced at the expense of other peoples, not by way of ignoring their fears. Let us therefore declare unequivocally that no solution shall be sought through a further revision of European frontiers. In the process of European rapprochement, frontiers should gradually lose much of their significance, but even this should not be regarded as an opportunity for the revival of nationalistic backsliding. While appreciating this fact, let us acknowledge openly the right of the Germans freely to decide on if or how they wish to unite their two states within their present frontiers. Following Bonn's agreements with its Eastern neighbors and the Helsinki accords, the signing of a peace treaty with Germany could become one of the most important levers for a positive transformation of Europe.

Another taboo subject has been the withdrawal of foreign troops. Let us therefore propose that the NATO and the Warsaw

Pact enter forthwith into negotiations on the dissolution of their military organizations, on the removal of all nuclear weapons either sited in or aimed at Europe, and on the withdrawal of US and Soviet troops from the territories of their European allies. Part of such an agreement should be the scaling down of armed forces in all countries of the European continent to a level eliminating the risk of aggression from any quarter.

These and other aims should be part and parcel of an interlocking process serving the ideal of mutual rapprochement and therefore offering no possible threat to any party. We do not seek to turn Europe into a third superpower, but instead, to overcome the superpower bloc structure by way of an alliance of free and independent nations within a democratic and self-governing all-European community living in friendship with nations of the entire world. The freedom and dignity of individual citizens are the key to the freedom and self-determination of nations. And only sovereign nations can transform Europe into a community of equal partners which would not pose the threat of a global nuclear war, but instead, serve as an example of real peaceful coexistence.

Perhaps this ideal sounds like a dream. However, we are convinced that it expresses the desire of a majority of Europeans. It is therefore an ideal worth striving for; all the more so, in view of the fact that today's world will hardly surmount its crisis unless Europe also takes the path its citizens desire.

We believe that our views will meet with your understanding, and we wish you every success in your proceedings.

Signed: Jarmila Belikova, Vaclav Benda, Tomas Bisek, Daniela

Biskova, Petr Cibulka, Jan Carnogursky, Albert Cerny, Jiri Dienstbier, Lubos Dobrovsky, Karel Freund, Jiri Hajek, Milos Hajek, Vaclav Havel, Ladislav Hejdanek, Oldrich Hromadko, Marie Hromadkova, Jirina Hrabkova, Jozef Jablonicky, Vladimir Kadlec, Eva Kanturkova, Bozena Komarkova, Jan Kozlik, Marie Rut Krizkova, Ladislav Lis, Jaromir Litera, Vaclav Maly, Anna Marvanova, Jaroslav Meznik, Pavel Murasko, Dana Nemcova, Radim Palous, Milos Rejchrt, Jakub Ruml, Jan Ruml, Jiri Ruml, Jan Sabata, Jaroslav Sabata, Anna Sabatova jr., Anna Sabatova sr., Libuse Silhanova, Jan Simsa, Petruska Sustrova, Petr Uhl, Vera Vranova, Josef Zverina.

Prague, March 11, 1985

This document was reprinted in East European Reporter, *Vol. 1, No. 1.*

APPENDIX II.

THE BERLIN APPEAL -- MAKE PEACE WITHOUT WEAPONS

1. There is only one kind of war that could still take place in Europe, nuclear war. The weapons stockpiled in the East and the West will not protect us, but destroy us. We will all be long dead when the soldiers in their tanks and at the missile base, as well as the generals and politicians in their bunkers, on whose protection we have relied, are still living and continuing to destroy whatever remains.

2. If therefore we want to remain alive -- away with the weapons! And first of all: away with the nuclear weapons. The whole of Europe must become a nuclear-weapons-free zone. We propose that there should be negotiations between the governments of the two German states about the removal of all nuclear weapons in Germany.

3. Divided Germany has become the deployment area for the two nuclear superpowers. We propose an end to this potentially fatal confrontation. The victors of World War II must finally conclude peace treaties with both German states, as decided in the Potsdam Agreement of 1945. Thereafter, the former Allies should withdraw their occupation troops from Germany and agree on guarantees of non-intervention in the internal affairs of the two German states.

4. We propose that the great debate about questions of peace be conducted in an atmosphere of tolerance and recognition of the

213

right of free expression, and that every spontaneous public manifestation of the desire for peace should be approved and encouraged. We appeal to the public and our government to discuss and reach decisions on the following questions:

a) Should we not renounce the production, sale and import of so-called war toys and games?

b) Should we not introduce lessons about problems of peace in our schools in place of "defense studies"?

c) Should we not allow a community peace service for conscientious objectors instead of the present kind of alternative military service?

d) Should we not renounce all demonstrations of military strength in public and instead use our national celebrations for declaring the people's desire for peace?

e) Should we not renounce so-called civil defense exercises? Since there is no possibility of meaningful civil defense in a nuclear war, these exercises simply play down the real nature of nuclear war. Is it not really a method of psychological preparation for war?

5. Make peace without weapons -- that does not only mean ensuring our own survival. It also means finishing with the senseless waste of labor and of the wealth of our people on the production of arms, and the equipping of gigantic armies of young people, who are thereby removed from productive work. Should we not rather be helping the starving all over the world instead of continuing to prepare for our own death?

Blessed are the meek:

for they shall inherit the earth.

(Jesus of Nazareth in the Sermon on the Mount)

The balance of terror has prevented nuclear war up to now only by postponing it until tomorrow. The peoples of the world regard the approach of this gruesome tomorrow with dread. They are searching for new ways to improve the foundations of peace. The "Berlin Appeal" is one expression of this search. Think about it, make proposals to our politicians, and everywhere discuss the question: What will bring about peace; what will bring about war?

Affirm your support for the "Berlin Appeal" by signing below.

Berlin, January 25, 1982

This document was reprinted in: John Sanford, The Sword and the Ploughshare: Autonomous Peace Initiatives in East Germany, and END Special Report, 1983.

APPENDIX III.

FREEDOM AND PEACE: DECLARATION OF PRINCIPLES

The Freedom and Peace movement was founded as an expression of the conviction that existing institutions and organizations fail to address issues and circumstances which people of good will should not ignore.

The struggle for human rights, for freedom of speech, press, and assembly, and for the freedom to organize associations is right and just. Right and just are the actions of the independent labor unions, which aim to protect workers from exploitation and injustice.

The Catholic Church, an institution of the highest authority, should be respected for its role as the representative and advocate of Polish national ideals and universal moral values. It is an indispensable part of the struggle for human rights to demand religious freedom, and to support the social and cultural initiatives connected with the Church.

The Freedom and Peace movement considers striving for national independence to be just. National oppression is an evil and eliminating it will lead to freedom for nations and will bring about peace among them.

The Freedom and Peace movement takes as its first foundation the struggle for human rights, religious freedom and national independence.

At the present time, the world faces the imminent threat of war, the consequences of which may be irreversible for human civilization. Many Poles are not aware of the reality of this threat, and treat it as an invention of communist propaganda.

Many Poles are not aware of the seriousness of the threat of nuclear war, of the problem of militarism and of a militaristic education. The second foundation of the Freedom and Peace movement is to change this situation.

Past experience indicates that political changes, though crucial, are unable to guarantee that love and truth will govern human relations.

The Freedom and Peace movement will disseminate knowledge which will enable man to understand human existence and man's place in the world. We will look to the attainment of Christian ethics, psychology, Eastern philosophies and other branches of learning which treat man as a subject.

This is the third foundation of the Freedom and Peace movement.

The Freedom and Peace movement takes non-violent resistance as its basic means of struggle against evil. Non-violence provides the most difficult, yet the most appropriate means for social struggle for human rights. It will be necessary to work out non-violent tactics which will be effective in a Communist totalitarian context.

We recognize that violence is morally justified in exceptional circumstances, for instance when life is endangered, particularly by mass extermination (e.g., the extermination of the Jews during World War II, or of the Cambodians under Pol Pot's regime).

Issues

I. Human Rights

The attainment of basic human rights, such as the freedom to express one's own ideas and opinions, the freedom to organize labor unions and other associations, and full religious freedom, provides the basis for deeper social change. The political system under which we live is characterized by perpetual violation and denial of these rights. Particularly important in this respect is the issue of prisoners' rights.

The Freedom and Peace movement wishes to concentrate on bringing about official recognition of the status of prisoners of conscience in Poland and throughout the world. The use of physical and psychological violence against prisoners is inadmissable. The Freedom and Peace movement will fight for the rights of prisoners, disseminate information about their situations and organize relief actions on their behalf.

We oppose capital punishment. Capital punishment is a disgrace of present day legal systems.

In these matters, we wish to unite our efforts with those of organizations and institutions that have similar goals, such as Amnesty International.

2. National Liberation

The Freedom and Peace movement will support the struggle of nations which have been the victims of the violence of foreign powers, be those powers national or ideological. It is unthinkable in the modern world that a nation which wishes to attain independence is politically prevented from doing so.

We support the efforts of ethnic groups and national minorities to achieve autonomy and greater control over their destiny.

The Freedom and Peace movement will demonstrate solidarity with those nations and minorities which demand their own rights.

We will support national minorities in Poland in their efforts to find an authentic institutional expression of their culture.

We will also take every opportunity to act on behalf of the rights of Poles who constitute a minority in other countries.

3. The Threat of War and the International Peace Movement

In view of the fact that the major threat to the modern world is nuclear annihilation, we will attempt to bring the enormity of this threat to the attention of Polish society. It is necessary to undo the currently militaristic character of education, both in the home and in the schools. It is time for the societies of East and West, which would find themselves adversaries in a future war, to undertake actions which would lead to dialogue and mutual understanding -- especially in view of the failed attempts to do so made by their governments. Of particular importance to us is establishing closer relations with Germany, a nation separated from us by the catastrophes of recent history, yet bound so closely to us by a common danger.

The Freedom and Peace movement considers the demilitarization of Central Europe and the creation of a nuclear-free zone there an absolute necessity. If accompanied by democratization of the East, this would decrease the danger of war.

At present, given the rift between the interests of the government and the aspirations of the Polish people, compulsory conscription violates people's consciences.

The Freedom and Peace movement plans to take action to change the text of the military oath, so that those who refuse to take it -- such as Marek Adamkiewicz -- would not face imprisonment for their beliefs.

Often military service is against an individual's moral, political or religious beliefs. The Freedom and Peace movement seeks to win the right for draftees in Poland to perform alternative civilian service which is not threatening to life. Such an arrangement exists in many other countries.

We respect and appreciate the work of many organizations and institutions for world peace. The Freedom and Peace movement wants to become an integral part of these efforts. Therefore, the expressions of support and solidarity conveyed to us by Western European peace organizations such as Comite pour le Desarmement Nucleaire en Europe (CODENE), Interkerkelijk Vredesberaad (IKV) and European Nuclear Disarmament (END) are very valuable.

We wish to work together with the international peace movement. Of particular importance to us in this collaboration is recognition of the basic truth that we will not successfully oppose war if we do not overcome political systems based on state violence against citizens. For us -- living in one such system -- this is the first and most important step toward universal peace. We wish to proceed along this path together with all the independent peace movements in Europe and in the world.

221

4. Environmental Protection

In the face of the growing threat of destruction of the biosphere, the air, the water and the soil, freedom should also mean this: the chance to live in an uncontaminated natural environment. At present, natural resources are being wasted, and the short-sighted policies of the authorities cause irreversible damage to the environment. Industry seeking to save on pollution-preventing devices is often the major cause of such damage. Poor management of natural resources leads to erosion of the soil, and the disappearance of forests and waters.

The Freedom and Peace movement will fight to make accessible information about the destruction of the natural environment.

Poland is not currently faced with the development of atomic energy plants. Nevertheless, industry's attempts to import nuclear technology -- after the experiences of other countries -- are a source of concern.

The Freedom and Peace movement will support those actions throughout the world whose aim is to safeguard the environment and ban nuclear testing.

5. World Hunger, Humanitarian Assistance

The Freedom and Peace movement considers hunger in the world today to be the greatest scandal of modern civilization. The demilitarization of Eastern Europe should serve not only to improve the fate of the Polish nation and her neighbors, but also to provide means of assistance to countries afflicted by poverty, famine and death.

222

Although charity cannot substitute for structural social change, this does not absolve us from providing volunteer assistance to those who are in need of it.

This applies to those suffering from poverty, sickness and loneliness in Poland.

The Freedom and Peace movement declares its willingness to cooperate with all organizations whose goal is to help the needy.

6. Human Development

Modern man faces several fundamental questions: What is the sense of human existence? How does one form and maintain relations with one's family and friends, as well as with people in general? How does one deal with personal and psychological problems?

The Freedom and Peace movement plans to organize and encourage lectures, publications and other means of helping people to find their own direction in life.

7. Tolerance

Within our movement, the basis for cooperation by people of differing world views is tolerance and understanding of the fact that there are many possible approaches to solving the world's problems.

We will be united by our opposition to evil, to oppression, to intolerance and to indifference to suffering.

The Freedom and Peace Movement
Gdansk, Krakow, Warsaw, Wroclaw
November 17, 1985
Machowa near Tarnow

This document was reprinted in <u>*Peace & Democracy News*</u>,
Summer-Fall 1986.

APPENDIX IV:

DECLARATION OF PRINCIPLES

GROUP TO ESTABLISH TRUST BETWEEN EAST AND WEST

The Group to Establish Trust Between the U.S. and the USSR (known as the Trust Group for short) is an independent group of peace advocates in the USSR which has existed since 1982. Its first task was to proclaim the intention to promote the establishment of mutual trust between the peoples of the USSR and the USA by organizing what we called the "four-sided dialogue between the USSR and USA," that is, having the independent societies of both countries join in the dialogue of the politicians on an equal-rights basis.

In the time since the Group was founded, its activity has been expanded by new aspects which have necessitated this document.

Peace and Mutual Trust

We believe that the reasons for the current tension in the world, fraught with universal nuclear destruction, are rooted in the lack of trust between countries and peoples. The way to eliminate this lack of trust and establish a stable peace, in our view, is to have the peoples of both countries come to know each other, change the manner in which people of another world view are treated, eradicate in people's consciousnesses the stereotype of the "enemy" imposed on them, and overcome the "barricade mentality." An important precondition for this is a belief in the essential absolute value of the human individual.

In order to realize these ideas it is essential to expand contacts between ordinary people in the East and West, eliminate governmental, political, ideological, and other barriers to East-West cooperation, and jointly resolve common problems. A cardinal increase is needed in the exchange of ideas, people and information in accordance with the spirit and letter of the Final Act of the Helsinki Conference on Security and Cooperation in Europe [signed by 35 nations in 1975 and known as the Helsinki Accords].

Therefore, we are appealing to the governments of the USSR, the USA and other countries of the East and West with a call to take such measures as the following toward overcoming mistrust and humanizing international relations:

-- a tourist program for inexpensive travel in the countries of the West and East by exchanging homes;

-- a program that would enable people to receive books and subscribe to journals both from the West and from the East;

-- a program to exchange children between Soviet and Western families during school holidays;

-- exchange of hired workers;

-- exchange of a network of permanent cultural centers;

-- television discussion between the politicians of both sides during which television viewers from West and East would have the opportunity to address questions to them over the telephone;

-- clinics for joint medical practice;

-- joint musical festivals for young people;

...and much, much more.

We see our purpose as follows:

-- to break down anti-Western sentiments and to oppose the expressions of xenophobia and chauvinism in our country;

-- to cooperate closely with activists in the peace movements abroad in order to overcome the mistrust towards the peoples of the USSR both in the West and in the Third World and in countries allied with the USSR;

-- to oppose the growing militarism of public consciousness, first of all, the system of so-called "military-patriotic education of youth";

-- to implant in the cultural ethos of society the anti-militaristic raising of children as an essential element of the humanization of social mores.

Taking into consideration all the complexities of contemporary international relations, we nevertheless are in principle opposed to the presence of foreign troops in foreign territories, first of all, the presence of Soviet troops in Afghanistan.

It should be emphasized in particular that we do not set as the goal of our activity the promotion of any government in winning for itself trust in the international arena, including the government of our own country. We believe that only the efforts of an independent [nepodkontrolnoye] society, of the ordinary peoples of the East and West, can guarantee the establishment of a climate of trust and a stable peace. Genuine detente is possible only from below, through the growth of a world-wide revolution of grass-roots peace initiatives.

Human Rights and Peace

These two issues, in our view, are inseparably linked. It is impossible to speak about peace without also discussing human rights issues. In the same way, it is unacceptable to be involved with the struggle for human rights while relegating to second place the problem of preserving peace, and ultimately, the survival of humankind. This principle is laid down in particular in the Helsinki Accords.

Peace in the world and peace within society depend on one another in the most intimate fashion. On the one hand, irreproachable observance by the authorities of human rights cannot help but have an impact on the elimination of mistrust in the international arena. The mistrust that is experienced towards a government that violates human rights is also extended towards ordinary citizens. Observance of these rights by governments will further the development of trust between peoples. On the other hand, trust-building measures between peoples and putting into practice "detente from below" will inevitably promote the normalization of the climate of international relations as well. For those of us who are living in the USSR, this is particularly important.

While advocating human rights as well as peace, it is impossible to limit oneself to any one country. The world is indivisible just as humanity is indivisible. Therefore, we are for

228

opposing all violations of human rights in any corner of the globe.

In our own country we consider the following to be essential:

    -- irreproachable adherence to the constitutional rights and freedoms of citizens;

    -- an amnesty for all prisoners of conscience, that is, persons deprived of their freedom because of their convictions, if they did not use or advocate violence;

    -- changes in the legislative and judicial-executive practices in the USSR with the objective of preventing opportunities for the persecution of people for their convictions;

    -- complete abolition of the death penalty;

    -- guarantee of the "right to pacifism," that is, establishment of alternative civilian service for persons who are unable, for reasons of conscience, to serve in the army;

    -- excercise to the fullest extent of the right to freedom of movement and choice of residence both outside one's country (unimpeded departure and return) and within one's country (the dismantling of the system of obligatory residence permits).

While noting the internal political aspect of the problem of trust, we also insist here the necessity for the free [nepodkontrolnaya] circulation of ideas and information, since the prolonged absence of freedom of information inside our country leads to a gulf of misunderstanding among entire groups of the population.

Protection of the Environment, Problems of the Third World, and Domestic Problems

The problems of preventing a world-wide ecological catastrophe have never been more critical. The immense resources which are presently being spent on producing the newest types of weapons could be successfully applied to resolve these ecological problems.

By the same token, joint international programs to meet world needs could serve as the most effective means of establishing trust in the world.

By cutting military expenditures, many internal problems could be dealt with in the USSR, for example, the food shortages, the housing problem, and women's issues. A radical improvement in the social security system could be made, particularly for disabled and elderly.

The problems of conserving the environment are as severe in the USSR as in any of the other developed industrial countries. Therefore, we oppose not only the military but the ecological threat, in particular, the industrial pollution of our atmosphere, soil and water. We also oppose agricultural methods that can lead to irreversible ecological damage as well as the plunderous exploitation of the natural resources of the animal and plant world.

The catastrophe at the Chernobyl nuclear power station which was unprecedented in scale, forced us to re-evaluate the dangers ensuing not only from nuclear weapons, but from atomic reactors used for peaceful means. In this connection we feel it is essential, at a minimum:

  -- to review all current programs of atomic energy for the purpose of adopting more effective safety measures.
  -- to shut down and cease construction of any new reactors of the RBMK type.
  -- to guarantee the accessibility [transparentnost] of atomic energy to international oversight by both governments and publics.
  -- to allocate additional resources for the creation of alternative non-nuclear energy sources (sun, wind, tides).

Conclusion

The Trust Group is an informal association of citizens who share the above principles. It is not an organization and does not presuppose "party discipline," or strict membership, or the presence of a leader. It does not have an obligatory program of action. The degree of activity of each person is determined by himself or herself, both concerning actions taken in the framework of the Group as well as actions taken individually, by one's own desire. By the same token, the degree of responsibility the Group takes for each of its activists is determined separately in each concrete instance.

In its activity, the Trust Group tries to cooperate to the maximum degree both with Western peace movements as well as unofficial movements of peace activists in the countries of Eastern Europe. Only by joint efforts can we build a stable, just and secure world, a world without war, violence or oppression.

Moscow
April 1987

ON INTERNATIONAL GLASNOST

At a time when the Soviet leadership is assuring us that it is striving for *glasnost* [public disclosure] in our country, we, members of the independent peace movement in the USSR, consider it necessary to make known the fact that a critical lack of such an approach is evident when it comes to international *glasnost*.

We cannot be completely satisfied with a situation where our population is offered information that is at times unexpectedly critical about domestic problems at the same time that the previous monopoly of the ruling ideology continues to be maintained over the coverage and interpretation of international events.

It is necessary to guarantee the right of ordinary people to become acquainted with the presentation of events and commentaries about international issues that differ from the presentation by the government. Such alternative presentations could overcome the confrontational thinking which often arises from one-sided presentation of information.

Such tendentiousness dictated by ideological tenets frequently incites in the masses a negative attitude toward the rival state in the overall context of detente. The saturation of the mass media with materials that do not coincide with the government's point of view creates a favorable climate for the eradication of the dangerous psychology of "the islanders" living under hostile encirclement.

Since the Soviet Union has a wide-scale penetration of information into the Western countries, a guarantee is required for equal conditions for the Western mass media in the USSR. A removal of the bans on the use of individual dish antennae and on the import of video cassettes and journals in the languages of the peoples of the USSR; the end of jamming of Western radio stations and the creation by ordinary citizens of independent information agencies (perhaps on a cooperative basis); the widespread sale of Western publications -- all of these would bring us closer to a united, renewed world, not divided into opposing military political blocs.

Moscow
May 22, 1987

Signed:

Alexander Rubchenko, Nikolai Khramov, Andrei Krivov, Irina Krivova, Yevgeniya Debryanskaya, Yekaterina Podoltseva, Alexander Zaitsev, Mikhail Kopot, Ivan Kopot, Yury Kiselyov, Aleksey Zvereyev, Kirill Popov, Mikhail Chertovskaya, Yelena Afanasyeva, Svetlana Yurlova, Stepan Gura, Rimma Aronova, Marina Yevich, Vladimir Pelikh, Dmitry Eisner, Irina Bayeva, Alexander Feldman, Grigory Yakobson, Vsevolod Filipyev, A. Verashchagin, Alexander Shoykhet, Anna Kopot

APPENDIX V:

DECLARATION OF PROTEST

which we are sending to the Slovenian, Yugoslav and Soviet Governments.

1. We severely CONDEMN the actions taken by the Soviet government following the Chernobyl accident, an accident which has and for a long time to come will have frightening consequences not unlike those of a nuclear bomb.

    a. because it consciously concealed the accident and first disclosed news only after alarm systems in other European countries were triggered. Their diplomatic representatives behaved cynically before all of world public opinion, claiming they delayed the release of information because the accident occurred on a non-working day;

    b. because of incomplete information and an information blockade which prevented the governments of the endangered countries from taking the necessary safety precautions;

    c. because of the inhuman attitude towards its own population which had to demonstrate with May Day celebrations, sports events etc., that life was proceeding normally and consequently the Chernobyl accident was nothing to worry about;

    d. because foreign citizens in the affected area at the time of the accident were not informed about what was really going on.

2.   We DEMAND of the Soviet government that in the future it make public all information relevant to effective protection against the consequences of such accidents and to possible neutralization of their consequences.

3.   We CONDEMN every attempt by the advocates of nuclear energy to depict the Chernobyl accident as a natural catastrophe and to deceive the public about the risks involved, because such risks are unavoidably and inseparably connected with the use of nuclear energy. We CONDEMN the prejudiced belittling and undervaluation of the danger of this and other similar accidents.

4.   We CONDEMN the abuse of the accident for propaganda purposes in the context of ideological warfare by any country or statesman.

5.   We DEMAND an immediate and unilateral halt to all nuclear testing. We REJECT all manipulation of international public opinion for propaganda purposes, such as one sided moratoria on nuclear testing, arming for peace, etc.

6.   We DEMAND that the Yugoslav government register a diplomatic protest to the government of the USSR over the tardy and incomplete release of information to the world.

7.   We strongly PROTEST and CONDEMN the way in which our republican governments informed the public of the danger of the Chernobyl accident and of the danger of its consequences for all of us:

> a. The public was not informed of the present danger immediately following the alarms but instead had to wait a day longer. Because of this we were exposed to the first and also the most dangerous

radioactive rain without knowing about it or being able to take even the most rudimentary safety measures. This delay in informing the public deserves additional condemnation because rainfall was predicted;

b. the most potentially endangered categories of the population were not publicly warned of the dangers of being outside during the heightened radiation (in addition to pregnant women and children, individuals suffering from specific ailments should at least have been warned);

c. doctors were not informed of the strength or composition of radioactivity, potentially leading to mistaken decisions on X-rays, chemotherapy, etc.;

d. information on the dangers of radiation was inadequate and contradictory, as was information on necessary safety and precautionary measures (different messages on the dangers of moving outdoors, of eating fresh vegetables, fruit and eggs, drinking milk, use of rain water etc.);

e. the public was not sufficiently acquainted with either the data on absolute strength or with the type of radiation, nor with the measures and criteria for the judgment of their danger.

8. We DEMAND that those responsible for the initial delay of information be located and that adequate sanctions be taken against them. We DEMAND that the public be informed of this.

9. For the future we DEMAND that the public be informed of all the dangerous consequences of Chernobyl and of all the

necessary and recommended safety measures. We WARN that any delay or cosmetic job on information for fear of "alarming the public" means irresponsible play with the lives and health of the people, for which no excuse exists in political or ideological factors.

10. We DEMAND that the executive government of the parliament of the Socialist Republic of Slovenia form a committee to estimate the damage and claim compensation from the government of the USSR at a relevant international court.

11. We DEMAND that details of the Yugoslav nuclear program be made public and the technical specifications and the anticipated domestic and foreign partners be disclosed. The Union of Associations for the Protection of the Environment of Slovenia must, in the context of the Socialist Alliance, prepare a conference which will re-examine those areas of the long-range program for the socio-economic development of Yugoslavia which deal with the construction of the four new nuclear plants.

12. We DEMAND that the Yugoslav parliament declare a moratorium on the building of nuclear plants.

13. We demand that a referendum be carried out immediately in Slovenia to democratically decide FOR or AGAINST the Prevlaka nuclear plant.

14. We DEMAND the formation of independent professional bodies to exercise control over all aspects of the use of nuclear energy in our country.

- Ljubljana May 10, 1986

This Declaration of Protest was reprinted from <u>*Across Frontiers*</u>, *Fall 1986, Vol.3, Nos. 1 & 2.*

GIVING REAL LIFE TO THE HELSINKI ACCORDS

A memorandum to citizens, groups and governments of all countries participating in the Conference on Security and Cooperation in Europe (CSCE)

PREFACE

The idea of this memorandum was launched by the European Network for East-West Dialogue which was founded in Perugia in 1984 to promote an exchange of opinions and experiences and common activities in a loose form of cooperation between peace groups in the West and independent groups, initiatives and individuals in the East.

The *Prague Appeal* which was signed in 1985 by a large number of Charter 77 signatories provided an important stimulus. This appeal which the Czechoslovak human rights initiative sent to the 4th Convention for European Nuclear Disarmament (END) in Amsterdam, emphasized the importance of the CSCE process for overcoming the division of Europe.

Work on the text lasted nearly one year with participation of groups and individuals from more than a dozen countries in East and West. In the course of long and sometimes difficult discussions among people with widely differing views and priorities, agreement on a number of common ideas and demands was eventually reached. It was a process of rapprochement and mutual learning.

This memorandum is not and does not intend to be a complete programme nor a common strategy. Rather it is a contribution to the all-European debate and it suggests steps towards a more comprehensive detente. We hope that this text will help to start a new round of discussions in the framework of the East-West dialogue.

Of course, endorsement of this memorandum need not necessarily mean agreement with every detail in the text, merely support for its general line and its main demands.

European Network for East-West Dialogue
November 1986

INTRODUCTION

Eleven years ago the final document of the Conference on Security and Cooperation in Europe was signed in Helsinki. Yet, today our continent is no more secure than in 1975 and cooperation is still endangered by a policy of confrontation. Many of the goals to which the governments committed themselves in Helsinki have remained dead letters. The militarization of societies continues. Communication between East and West is hampered by many barriers. Both East and West reproduce enemy images that constitute a threat to peace. Basic civil rights still do not exist in many of the CSCE countries.

Those who live in a divided Europe have a fundamental interest in seeing that the Helsinki process results in something tangible. In this memorandum we, citizens of CSCE countries, present some of our own ideas and proposals to the public and to the government representatives meeting for the CSCE review conference in Vienna in November 1986. We do this as rightful actors in the framework of the Helsinki Accords that explicitly envisage cooperation between individuals, groups and societies as an important contribution to the implementation of the goals proclaimed in Helsinki.

For us, the three "baskets" of the Helsinki Final Act are interdependent. We oppose any tendency to play off peace against freedom or vice versa. A lasting detente cannot be bought at the cost of playing down the question of civil liberties and human – political and social – rights. Peace and security, detente and cooperation, basic rights and self-determination of peoples have to be achieved all together. Set-backs in any of these spheres have their negative effects on all others.

We are aware that the Helsinki Accords do not provide satisfying answer to some of the most pressing problems of today such as the ever-widening rift between rich industrialized nations and Third World countries, the impending destruction of our natural environment and the destructive effects of some forms of industrial and technological progress. Even though we cannot discuss these questions in detail they provide for us a necessary background for reflection and for political action in the framework of the CSCE process.

The growing contacts between independent and autonomous groups and individuals in East and West in recent years, and our common experience in developing a dialogue from below, have strengthened our conviction that more initiatives, proposals, and pressure from citizens and non-governmental organizations are required to revitalize the CSCE process.

In our view we need a new concept for a detente policy which should include the following elements:
– Peoples and governments of all CSCE countries need to recognize their own responsibility for solving the most urgent problems of our continent. Europeans should no longer look only to the superpowers and to bloc-to-bloc negotiations for providing solutions, but rather should try to develop their own initiatives and to strengthen existing tendencies towards a plurality of relationships between states in East and West.
– Detente policy, to achieve permanent results, must have a firm basis not only on the governmental level, but within societies. Grass roots contacts and common

activities between groups and individuals across frontiers can dissolve the structure of Cold War and prepare the ground for "Hot Peace". Official detente policy should create a framework which encourages the process of "detente from below".

Stability in international relations also rests on the independent and democratic development of societies. Indeed such a development is urgently needed. Peace on our continent can only be secure if it is a really democratic peace, based on civil liberties and social justice, and is, thus, wholeheartedly supported and defended by all European citizens. In our view the implementation of basic civil rights – such as freedom of thought and of conscience, freedom of assembly and association, and freedom of information – is an ongoing condition:
- for societies to be able to respond to important issues and to exercise democratic control over their own governments;
- for communication, cooperation, and all forms of exchange between East and West to become more meaningful;
- for safeguarding disarmament and a stable, lasting and democratic peace on our continent.

To prevent a war in Europe obviously is a necessary condition for progress in any field.

We reject the use of military and para-military forces or secret service activities to suppress social changes within a country as well as any interference by such forces or threats of such interference into the internal affairs of other countries. At the same time we strongly advocate trans-frontier solidarity, mutual support and cooperation between people and groups working for peace, civil liberties, trade union rights, social justice, women's emancipation, or ecological goals. In our view such activities are an essential contribution to our common efforts to build a new peaceful and democratic Europe.

DETENTE FROM BELOW

Mutual trust cannot be created solely by governments. It must be built up between citizens as well. All those who want to promote the Helsinki principles should, in our view, not only try to mobilize public opinion in order to put pressure on governments. They also ought to think about what they can do themselves to further develop detente from below and to build bridges across the rift dividing our continent.

Forty years of separation and living in very different social realities have created a deep mutual alienation between Europeans on both sides of the rift. Even geographic terms seem to have changed their meaning. People in the West often speak of "Europe" when, in fact, they mean the member countries of the EEC. On the other hand terms like "East" and "West" are used in a rather loose political sense. Thus countries which by geography as well as political and cultural tradition belong to Central rather than to Eastern Europe find that they are considered as part of "the East".

To rediscover together an all-European context and perspectices, people from all parts of this continent should, wherever possible, try to meet and to talk to each other. There are many ways to deepen contacts, once they are established: invitations on an individual basis and pen pals; pupil and student exchanges as well as scientific, cultural and sport exchanges; mutual visits between youth and vocational organizations, trade unions, churches and all kinds of popular music groups; twinning of towns. Many of these activities can be arranged outside of or in addition to official programmes.

Representatives of political parties, trade unions, churches and other institutions in the West should use the opportunity of visits to Eastern Europe to meet both representatives of official or semi-official organizations and activists in independent groups. Of course, in the East there is a fundamental difference between independent groups and organizations and institutions which all have an official or semi-official character.

In our view, it is of special importance to widen and intensify the dialogue and the cooperation between independent and autonomous groups in East and West working for peace, human right issues and ecological goals. The existence and activities of these groups make an indispensable contribution to detente from below.

We demand the right of unhampered action for all such groups in all CSCE countries. This includes the right to exchange experiences with like-minded groups across all frontiers, the right to attend international meetings and conferences, and the possibility to organize trans-frontier activities on peace and on environmental protection. People involved in different types of grass roots activities should know that they can expect our active support and solidarity whenever they are subjected to repressive acts.

As practical steps to promote detente from below we suggest:
- Establishment of a fund to be raised and administered by non-governmental groups and organizations for supporting East-West holiday camps for young people with common interests like music, sport, ecology, study of the same language etc.
- Establishment of a non-governmental monitoring agence – promoted by the CSCE – to analyse the work and progress of the CSCE process and to submit practical proposals. Such an agency should consist of representatives of national and international peace research institutes and of other relevant scientific institutions, of representatives of a wide spectrum of peace, civil rights and other citizens' groups in East and West and should be able to rely on the support of a large panel of experts in all relevant fields.

EUROPEAN SECURITY

Peace is more than the absence of war. A lasting peace can only be obtained by overcoming the various political, economic, and social causes of aggression and violence in international relations as well as in the internal affairs of states. A comprehensive democratization of states and societies would create conditions favorable to this aim. Such democratization includes the existence of a critical public which has the capacity to exercise effective control over all aspects of military and security policy.

The more citizens in all parts of our continent consider peace as their own personal concern and try to influence governments, institutions and political parties, the more it will be possible to promote common security interests in all CSCE countries. When the fate of all Europe, and indeed of all mankind, is at stake, the peoples and governments of countries threatened by nuclear annihilation have the moral right and the obligation to make every conceivable political effort in order to intervene in the decision-making process.

If we are to move towards a stable peace order, we have to reject the main tenets of present security doctrines. Many governments and politicians argue that nuclear war can be prevented by preparing for it. We think that this is an irresponsible argument. The doctrine of nuclear deterrence, adhered to on both sides, is a driving force in the ongoing arms race. Lasting peace cannot be based on the threat of mutual annihilation.

Measures of arms control are not sufficient to remove the grave dangers inherent in the present situation. Security in Europe can only be achieved if the tremendous number of all kinds of weapons concentrated on our continent is drastically reduced. The arsenals of the superpowers must be substantially curtailed. France and Britain with their nuclear potentials as well as every CSCE country must also be prepared to contribute to a general process of disarmament. We strongly oppose any proposal to establish Western Europe as a third military or even nuclear superpower. This would only increase the danger of war and the rift dividing our continent.

Security, in our view, can emerge only from the insight that establishing peace is a common task in which governments and peoples of all CSCE countries must cooperate as partners with equal rights. What is needed to achieve this common task is a whole package of interrelated political as well as military measures: measures to promote detente from above and below, to establish mutual trust and to reverse tendencies of militarization of societies; measures to prevent an arms race in space and to reduce armaments of all levels, including nuclear, chemical, biological and conventional weapons; agreements on the reduction of troops and on a drastic reduction of arms exports. A credible and democratic control and verification of all such measures would be very important.

To overcome the blinkers of thinking only in terms of the balance of military power we suggest that people wanting to promote peace ought to consider – in East and West – independent steps of disarmament and trust building measures. At the same time possibilities for different forms of strictly defensive military strategies ought to be explored.

The following steps are suggested in the hope that governments and politicians will take them into serious consideration. Whether they can be achieved depends largely upon the engagement and mobilization of citizens in East and West.

– The withdrawal and dismantling of all medium range missiles and of all nuclear weapon systems with short warning time stationed in or directed at targets in Europe.
– A comprehensive test ban treaty adhered to by all CSCE countries.
– A total ban on the production and stockpiling of chemical, biological and environmental weapons in Europe and elsewhere in the world.
– The establishment of zones free of nuclear weapons without increases in conven-

tional armament.
- An agreement between all CSCE countries to reduce their military expenditures proportionally. Savings accruing in this way should go into a common CSCE fund for financing development projects especially in the Third World.
- Official publication of military budgets, complete and regular information on all military planning as well as on the individual contributions of the Eastern and Western countries to the military alliances.
- Campaigns in East and West against all forms of domestic militarism. Abolition of military instruction in schools and universities as well as of para-military training. Initiatives for a comprehensive peace education and for independent research on peace.
- Limitations on the length of compulsory military service to not more than one year in all CSCE countries.
- Recognition of the right to refuse military service for reasons of conscience as a basic human right in all CSCE countries; provision of an alternative form of civilian service.

Activities in support of any of these demands must be recognized as a basic democratic right in all CSCE countries.

HUMAN RIGHTS

Civil liberties and basic political rights like freedom of thought and conscience, freedom of assembly and organization, and freedom of information are guaranteed in the constitutions of all CSCE countries and they have been confirmed in the Helsinki Accords. Yet, the implementation of these rights in actual practice often is severely restricted or non-existent in many CSCE countries.

In the parliamentary democracies of Western Europe, civil liberties and basic political rights are, as a rule, respected. Nevertheless, there are repeated attempts in many of these countries to undermine these rights and to erode democracy. It is possible to detect tendencies towards a "surveillance-state". Many important political, economic and especially military issues are removed from the ordinary process of democratic decision-making. Foreigners living and working in these countries are often discriminated against both by official institutions and by large parts of the population. A growing number of people and groups are becoming socially marginalized.

People who live in the Eastern half of Europe, as a rule, are not able to resist the inadequate or non-existent implementation of their formally acknowledged basic rights. There is not even an institutionally recognized means to express their demands, interests and goals or to exercise democratic control over those in power. Such a state of affairs leads to continuous discontent with prevailing conditions and creates an ever-present source of tension inside societies which adversely affects East-West relations. All this, in fact, constitutes a stumbling bloc in the process of effective detente.

In our view, working for civil liberties and social rights is not only a moral obligation for everyone cherishing human dignity and democratic ideals, but also a political necessity if we want to create the conditions for a stable, lasting and democratic peace.

We reject all kinds of double standards for East and West in the application of basic rights and demand the full implementation of the whole catalogue of human rights as listed in the Helsinki Final Act and in the International Convenants on Political and Civil Rights and on Cultural, Economic and Social Rights in all CSCE countries. This also includes the right to form independent trade unions and to practise religious without hindrance.

Urgent first steps for the immediate future should include:

– Freedom of travel between all CSCE countries, without any need for special exit permission from one's own country and with guaranteed right to return. No restrictions on contact with foreigners.
– Freedom of mobility within one's country.
– Right of emigration for all citizens of all Helsinki countries without loss of personal property and without discrimination such as having to pay a huge ransom under the pretext of refunding for schooling or professional education.
– Recognition of the existence of an independent editing and publishing sector.
– No restriction on the transport of books, tapes, journals etc. across frontiers as long as they are the personal property of the traveller.
– The right of national and ethnic minorities to their own schools, autonomous cultural activities, and adequate representation in all public offices.
– Consideration of the proposal to acknowledge the status of political prisoners for people convicted for exercise of their civil rights and political beliefs.
– The immediate release of all political prisoners who in their activities have never used or advocated any form of violence.
– Abolition of all kinds of "Berufsverbote" (professional restrictions) as applied in many countries in East and West and of the practice, widespread in the East, of imprisoning people solely for being unemployed for political or non-political reasons.
– Abolition of the death penalty in all CSCE countries.

Moreover, we suggest the establishment of an all-European commission of human rights to which citizens of all CSCE countries and people from other continents living in these countries have a guaranteed legal right of appeal if they feel that their basic rights have not been respected.

ECONOMIC AND ECOLOGICAL COOPERATION

Whatever their social structure, countries in both East and West are at present committed to undifferentiated, quantitative economic growth. Everywhere there seem to be inbuilt mechanisms that promote the reckless squandering of natural as well as of technical and scientific resources. One of the major factors of waste of both material resources and scientific and technical know-how is the ongoing arms race. About half of the research efforts in West, East and South is devoted to purely destructive purposes. Military-industrial complexes, existing in both East and West, exert strong pressures to maintain and accelerate the arms race and are increasingly becoming dominant factors in economic life.

World wide detente and disarmament would not only facilitate an improvement in conventional East-West economic relations. It would also create the pre-conditions for an economic policy requiered to solve our social and environmental problems in the CSCE countries and to give real and effective aid to developing countries.

If economic activity is to serve human wellbeing and to improve our quality of life new priorities need to be set in East and West. New efforts must be made to find a proper balance between economic growth, the aim of social equality, and ecological requirements. Economic activity must in its daily practice take into consideration the fact that natural resources are limited, that our environment must be adequately protected, and that in the context of new technological developments the future status of human labour needs to be redefined. To our knowledge neither of the rival systems in Europe has so far been able to propose viable solutions to all these grave problems.

The economic systems in East and West urgently need democratization. Social needs such as housing or work in safe and human conditions have to become more important in defining economic priorities. In the West a primary task is to ensure that people are no longer marginalized by massive unemployment. In the East, decentralization of the economy is an essential task in order to make the economy more efficient and responsive to the needs of the people.

We are rather sceptical about the trend prevailing today in all parts of the world of concentrating very much effort on large, prestigious and expensive industrial and technological projects while at the same time there is a dire lack of material and human resources for the most urgent tasks like eradicating hunger or solving the pressing social and environmental problems existing in West, East and South.

We think that a re-evaluation of nuclear technology is necessary not only because of the lessons to be drawn from the Chernobyl catastrophe, but also because of the problems of proliferation of nuclear weapons. We propose that no new nuclear power stations be commissioned and that concrete plans with specific time limits for a speedy phasing out of nuclear energy be drawn up. In particular we strongly oppose a move towards a plutonium economy, we oppose fast breeder reactors and commercial reprocessing. We demand intensive efforts to reduce any squandering of energy and generous funding to promote alternative energy sources.

We are disturbed by the present trend towards ever more unequal trade relations between East and West. For various reasons Eastern industrial products continually lose market shares in the West. Exports from the East increasingly consist of raw materials and energy. The technological gap between West and East is increased. In our view, this trend cannot serve the long term economic interests of any CSCE country. Agreements on cooperation between EEC, EFTA, COMECON and the USA therefore should help to reduce the structural problems in economic relations between East and West.

In order to promote economic and ecological cooperation between East and West we suggest the following practical steps:
- Establishment of a CSCE development fund to support programmes for improving economic structure in industry, agriculture and transport in economically weak regions and for measures to protect the environment.
- Speedy implementation of international cooperation in matters of environmental protection, in particular to achieve a drastic reduction of both internal and trans

246

frontier air and water pollution.
- Increasing cooperation between East and West in projects of economic and technical assistance to the Third World countries (national and sub-national).
- Convocation of CSCE forums on economic cooperation and ecological problems with the participation of both official representatives and independent experts, including experts from citizens' groups, trade unions and consumer organizations.
- Establishment of a permanent independent commission – promoted by the CSCE – to investigate and measure ecological damage and to propose action. All information and proposals produced by this commission should be published openly in all CSCE countries.

CULTURAL COOPERATION

European identity is based on a collective memory of a shared history and culture. The roots of European identity go much deeper than the recent historical events of the last forty years or even this century. Europe is more than the Western European Community, a Western or an Eastern bloc.

Eurpean civilisation was built on a pluralism of cultures from within and outside Europe. And yet Europe has often failed to respect other cultures, forcibly imposing its own culture on other parts of the world. Europeans have a responsibility to avoid an exclusive and egocentric sense of identity.

Among the many elements which make up the cultural heritage shared by the peoples of Europe are antique and Judaeo-Christian tradition, Roman law, the ideas of enlightenment, and liberal, democratic and socialist thinking. European civilization is inseperably bound up with the notion of freedom of the individual and of a civil society as different from the state. This notion is an important condition for citizens to be able to express full commitment and responsibility for the development of the whole of society.

Historical experiences bound up with suppression, war and extermination are part of the common history and thus of the collective memory of European peoples. The consequences of these shared experiences are an aversion to another war on this continent, a wish for cooperative coexistence, and a growing awareness that respect for human rights, both civil and socio-economic is basic to such cooperation.

In Europe's culture the shared history and the experiences of its peoples, their hopes, disappointments, disastrous errors, as well as some unkept promises and unachieved utopias, all find their expression. Cultural activity therefore is an important field for Europeans to confront themselves with their history and unite in searching for a common future.

Many West Europeans tend to perceive themselves primarily as members of the Atlantic community. Within the last decades they have responded only by silence to the consistent attempts to isolate the peoples of the Eastern half of this continent form the other half's cultural life. As all Europeans have a stake in our common heritage, West Europeans ought to overcome their indifferent and inward looking attitude by opening themselves towards the culture of their fellow Europeans and by providing full support to them.

The Helsinki Accords and the later CSCE agreements created some useful framework for cultural exchange between East and West that need to be further developed. Most important is to provide space for independent cultural and scientific activity. All those working in these fields ought to be able to develop forms of cooperation autonomously within their countries and across frontiers.

As useful steps for the near future we suggest:

- The establishment of an all-European cultural foundation to promote cultural exchange on all levels and to finance and organize common projects like exhibitions, film and theatre festivals, and literary colloquia. The active participation of artists and writers in such a cultural foundation should be guaranteed.
- Bilateral and multilateral agreements to facilitate the study of European languages and literatures; providing funds for the translation and dissemination of the literatures of the smaller European peoples; creation of a "European library" in which important works of all European literatures are regularly and simultaneously published in East and West.
- Abolition of all forms of censorship wherever they exist, in particular for works of science and culture. Free access to foreign scientific and literary works in all libraries.
- Exchange of television and radio programmes and free exchange of books and journals between all CSCE countries.
- Joint scientific and literary projects to investigate and overcome prejudices and enemy images, including continuation of work by existing and future joint commissions on school books and other teaching materials.
- CSCE exchange programmes for scientists and teachers. Twinnings of scientific and cultural institutions from Eastern and Western Europe whereby non-official and self-organized initiatives should not only be allowed, but encouraged.

THE EUROPE WE ENVISAGE

The Helsinki Accords are often presented as confirming the status quo in Europe. Yet they do not in letter or spirit cement the bipolar structure of power blocs. These Accords confirm the territorial status quo in Europe and reject the use of force in international relations. Yet they leave the door open for peaceful and gradual change towards a pluralistic Europe which can overcome the bloc structure. The neutral and non-aligned countries whose proposals and initiatives have substantially promoted the CSCE process can play a vital role in helping Europe to escape from bipolarity.

Whether the future of Europe will remain squeezed into the bipolar strait-jacket or whether our continent will be gradually able to liberate itself form these constraints depends to a large extent on the will and the ability of Europeans in East and West to clearly articulate their own interests vis-a-vis the superpowers and on political and social change within the superpowers themselves. We are aware of the fact that the Europe which we strive for cannot be built in confrontation with or by exclusion of either the USA or the Soviet Union, but only in a common effort of all CSCE countries. People and governments of this continent have to search for viable compromises with both leading powers.

If such a long term project is to become a realistic alternative to the status quo, if in other words we are to radicalize the Helsinki process so as to make it part of a comprehensive democratic programme, then we must oppose those superpower policies which contravene the right of countries to self-determination. All independent groups, movements and citizens' initiatives in East and West should deliberately put pressure on the superpowers to get them to abandon their hegemonic behaviour and start acting as democratic partners.

The Europe we envisage would consist of peoples and nations that are willing to live together as good neighbours. A Europe where all peoples have the possibility to organize their mutual relations as well as their internal political, economic and cultural affairs in a democratic and self-determined way. Within this perspective the two German states should put forward initiatives promoting the general process of detente as well as positive change in the relations between each other. It should be clear that the German question is a European one and therefore any effort to solve it should be part of a democratic programme to overcome the bloc structure in Europe.

The Europe we envisage will gain strength from its internal democracy and should be able to play an important role in international affairs. In particular, Europe needs to find ways to transform North-South relations and become a pace-setter for political equality and economic justice in dealing with the Third World. Such a Europe would oppose any form of military interventionism, like for example the present US actions in Central America or the Soviet invasion of Afghanistan.

We ask both politicians and the public to explore all possibilities for preparing the ground for a pluralistic, democratic and peaceful community of European nations acting as partners with equal rights and especially to consider a cluster of ideas and measures as outlined below:

- To facilitate and enhance an ongoing and widespread political dialogue between East and West on all levels which in its first stage will help to overcome the crisis in the Helsinki process.
- To give full support to all measures aimed at reducing tension between the superpowers and promoting detente and mutual trust between them. Furthermore, helping to blunt any aggressive posturing of the superpowers and especially to encourage, wherever necessary, thorough democratization of their policies.
- Establishment of a system of political, economic and cultural cooperation of all CSCE countries going beyond the present economic-political communities in East and West.
- A major reduction and finally a complete withdrawal of all foreign weapons and troops from all European countries, including the removal of all foreign military bases and facilities.
- The dissolution of NATO and Warsaw Pact and all other bilateral and multilateral military treaties between CSCE countries. This can be an essential step towards a common security system and will contribute to overcoming the division of Europe.
- A peace constitution for Europe based on full respect for the right of self-determination of all nations, which would transform the ten basic principles proclaimed in the Helsinki Accords into political reality, guaranteed by a treaty valid under international law.

FIRST SIGNATORIES OF THE MEMORANDUM „GIVING REAL LIFE TO THE HELSINKI ACCORDS"

Austria:
Dolores Bauer (member of the City Council of Vienna), Georg Breuer (journalist of sciences), Dr. Erhard Busek (vice-mayor of Vienna and official spokesperson on culture for the People's Party, ÖVP), Dr. Erich Fröschl (director of the Karl-Renner-Institute), Walter Geyer (MP for the Green-Alternative List), Dr. Heinz Gärtner (collaborator of the Institute for International Politics, Laxenburg), Dr. Josef Höchtl (MP for the ÖVP), Prof. Dr. Günther Hödl (pedagogue), Prof. Dr. Hoffmann-Ostenhof (biochemist, secretary of the Austrian Pugwash group), Dr. Peter Jankowitsch (MP for the SPÖ, former foreign minister), Premysl Janyr (journalist), Albrecht K. Konecny (editor-in-chief of the review „Zukunft") Dr. Hilde Koplenig (historian), Prof. Dr. Helmut Kramer (political scientist), Bishop Florian Kundtner (chairperson of the commission „Justitia et Pax" of the Austrian bishops' conference), Prof. Dr. Friedrich Levcik (economist, former director of the Vienna Institute for International Economic Comparisons), Freda Meißner-Blau (MP for the Green-Alternative List), Dr. Andreas Maislinger (collaborator of the Institute for Political Sciences, Innsbruck), Zdeněk Mlynář (political scientist, Listy-group), Prof. Dr. Ewald Nowotny (economist, MP for the SPÖ), Prof. Dr. Anton Pelinka (political scientist), Peter Pilz (MP for the Green-Alternative List), Prof. Hans Rotter (moral theologian), Kaspanaze Simma (member of the regional parliament of Vorarlberg for the Green-Alternative List), Prof. Dr. Walter Thirring (physicist), Helmut Strobl (member of the City Council of Graz, ÖVP), Andreas Wabl (MP for the Green-Alternative List), Dr. Erwin Waldschütz (collaborator of the Institute for Christian Philosophy at the University of Vienna), Dr. Erwin Wancata (spokesperson of the Catholic Student Youth in Vienna), Hans Weigel (writer), Prof. Dr. Erika Weinzierl (contemporary historian)

Belgium:
Bruno Coppieters (political scientist and peace activist), E. Corjn (trade unionist), Luc Deliens (sociologist and peace activist), Jean Van Lierde (chairperson of the European Bureau for Conscientious Objection), Ernest Mandel (economist), P. Pataer (Christian senator, associated with the fraction of the Flemish Socialist Party), Freddy de Pauw (journalist), François Roelants de Vivier (MEP for Ecolo), Paul Staes (MEP for Agalev), Patrick Stouthuysen (peace researcher)

Canada:
Bruce Allen (activist of the Auto-Workers Union and member of ACT for Disarmament, Niagara), Joanne Santa Barbara (MD, Canadian Physicians for the Prevention of Nuclear War), Prof. Ronald Balbin (Quebec Coalition for Disarmament and Peace), Jean-François Beaudet (Quebec Coalition for Disarmament and Peace), Stephen Darkowich (ACT for Disarmament, Toronto), David Delauney, Prof. Eric Fawcett (founding president of Science for Peace), George Ignatieff (president of

Science for Peace), Sister Mary Jo Leddy (Christian Peace Initiative), Prof. John Polanyi (University of Toronto, 1986 Nobel laureate – physical chemistry, UN Association), Dorothy Goldin Rosenberg (Voice of Women), Dimitrios Roussopoulos (writer, Quebec Coalition for Disarmament and Peace), Arnold Simoni (World Federalist), Frank Sommers (MD, founding president of Physicians for Social Responsibility), Prof. Metta Spencer (editor, Peace Magazine), Murray Thomson (Peace Fund Canada), Prof. Jean-Guy Vaillaincourt (Montreal University)

Czechoslovakia:
Luboš Bažant (labourer), Václav Benda (philosopher, mathematician, now stoker), Irena Boruvková (former journalist), Jiří Dienstbier (journalist, now stoker), Miklos Duray (member of the Committee for the Defense of the Hungarian Minority in Czechoslovakia), Jiří Hajek (historian, former Foreign Minister), Václav Havel (playwright), Ladislav Hejdánek (philosopher, now warehouse worker), Eva Kanturková (writer), Jindřich Kopaček (former university lecturer, now labourer), Jan Kozlik (Protestant minister deprived of state licence), Miroslav Kusý (writer, philosopher), Ladislav Lis (lawyer, former official of the Communist Party, now farm labourer), Václav Maly (Catholic priest deprived of state licence), Anna Marvanová (former journalist), Lenka Mullerová-Marečková (clerk, now unemployed, poet), Dana Němcová (psychologist, now on disability pension), Martin Palouš (computer programmer), Radim Palouš (philosopher), Miloš Rejchrt (Protestant minister, now stoker), Jiří Ruml (former journalist), Jan Sabata (hospital worker), Jaroslav Sabata (psychologist, former leading politician of the Prague Spring), Anna Sabatová (member of the Committee for the Defense of Unjustly Prosecuted, VONS), Milan Simečka (writer, philosopher), Jan Simsa (Protestant Minister deprived of state licence), Václav Slavík (former leading politician of the Prague Spring), Jan Stern (former journalist), Jarmila Stibicová (former teacher), Jaromir Stibic (clerk), Jakub Trojan (theologian and Protestant minister deprived of state licence, now labourer), Petr Uhl (member of VONS, former teacher, now stoker), Josef Zvěrina (Catholic philosopher) – (The majority of the above are Charter 77 signatories, 17 of them being former or current Charter 77 spokespersons.)

Denmark:
Ole Bertelsen (bishop of Copenhagen), Jørn Boye Nielsen (professor of the International People's College), Lasse Budtz (MP for the Social Democrats), Christian Ejlers (publisher), Niels Gregersen (doctor of medicine, University of Aarhus), Peter Hartoft Nielsen (collaborator of the Danish Ministry of the Evironment), Niels Hass (drama critic), Claus Jensen (international secretary of the General Workers' Union of Denmark), Preben Stuer Lauridsen (professor of law at the University of Copenhagen), Toni Liversage (writer), Peter Lodberg (general secretary of the Ecumenical Council of Denmark), Gunna Starck (mayor for town planning of Copenhagen), Arne Stinus (MP for the Social Liberal Party), Pelle Voigt (MP for the Social People's Party), Merete Voldstedlund (actress), Ole Waever (peace researcher), Judith Winther (East-West group of the movement "No to Nuclear Weapons")

Federal Republic of Germany/West Berlin:

Prof. Dr. Ulrich Albrecht (university professor, peace researcher), Lothar Baier (writer), Gerd Bastian (MP for the Green Party), Undine von Blottnitz (MEP for the Green Party), Dr. Peter Brandt (historian), Hans Christoph Buch (writer), Dr. Andreas Buro (university professor), Dany Cohn-Bendit (journalist), Peter Conradi (MP for the SPD), Dieter Esche (secretary of the "European Network for East-West-Dialogue"), Dr. Tilman Evers (coordinator for studies at the Evangelical Academy Hofgeismar), Tilman Fichter (political scientist), Uli Fischer (MP for the Green Party), Jürgen Fuchs (writer), Klaus Hänsch (MEP for the SPD), Dieter Hoffmann-Axthelm (writer), Milan Horaček (Green Party), Willi Hoss (MP for the Green Party), Ingrid Karsunke (editor of the review "Kursbuch"), Yaak Karsunke (writer), Petra Kelly (MP for the Green Party), Sarah Kirsch (writer), Lew Kopelew (writer), Peter Lohauß (member of the City Council of West Berlin, Alternative List), Prof. Dr. Wilfried Loth (historian), Prof. Dr. Adolf Müller (political scientist, Listy-group), Prof. Dr. Oskar Negt (sociologist), Wolfgang von Nostitz (lawyer, MEP for the Green Party), Prof. Dr. Peter von Oertzen (member of the presidium of the SPD), Prof. Dr. Michal Reiman (political scientist, Listy-group), Prof. Dr. Horst-Eberhard Richter (psychoanalyst), Dr. Fritz Riege (member of the regional parliament of Niedersachsen for the SPD), Heinke Salisch (MEP for the SPD), Wolfgang Schenk (member of the City Council of West Berlin, Alternative List), Otto Schily (lawyer, Green Party), Dr. Peter Schlotter (peace researcher), Renate Schmidt (MP and vice-chairwoman of the SPD in Bavaria), Joscha Schmierer (publicist), Peter Schneider (writer), Christian Semler (freelance journalist), Dr. Eva Senghaas-Knobloch (social and peace researcher), Johano Strasser (writer and editor of the review "L 80", SPD), Heinz Suhr (MP for the Green Party), Zoltan Szankay (university lecturer), Klaus Vack (secretary of the "Committee for Basic Rights and Democracy"), Klaus Wettig (MEP for the SPD), Inge Wettig-Danielmeier (member of the regional parliament of Niedersachsen, chairwoman of the working group of Socialdemocrat Women), Heidemarie Wieczorek-Zeul (MEP for the SPD)

France:

Didier Anger (ecologist), Etienne Balibar (philosopher), Karel Bartošek (historian, Listy-group), Denis Berger (university professor), Jacques Berthelet (publisher), Louisette Blanquart (trade unionist and feminist), Seweryn Blumsztajn (founding member of KOR in Poland, today leading position in the Foreign Bureau of Solidarność in Paris), Claude Bourdet (writer and journalist, former member of the National Council of the Résistance), Jean-Marie Brohm (professor of physiology), Michel Butel (writer), Jacques Chatagner (director of the review "Lettre"), Jean Chesneaux (historian), Yvan Craipeau (essayist), Philippe Deblock (president of the Christian Rural Youth), Bernard Dornig (economist), René Dumont (agrarian scientist), Jean-Jacques de Felice (lawyer, vice-president of the "League for Human Rights"), Mgr. Jacques Gaillot (bishop of Evreux), Mgr. Guy Herbulot (bishop of Corbeil), Felix Guattari (psychoanalyst), Albert Jacquard (biologist), Georges Labica (philosopher, university professor), Bernard Langlois (journalist), Denis Langlois (lawyer), Victor Leduc (university professor), Jean-Claude Lescornet (general secretary of PSU), Antonin Liehm (writer and editor of the review "Lettre Internationale"), Alain Lipietz (economist), Sylvie Mantrant (international secretary of the independent peace coordination CODENE), Guy Marimot (ecologist), Christian Mellon (Jesuit priest, peace researcher), Maurice Najman (journalist), Paul Noirot (publicist und co-editor of the review "Lettre Internationale"), Jean-Louis Peyroux (journalist), Emmanuel Raspe (economist), Bernard Ravenel (teacher), Daniel Richter (trade unionist), Antoine Sanguinetti (retired Admiral), Manuel Terray (social scientist), Jean-Pierre Vigier (physicist), Georges Waysand (physicist) – Group "Solidarity with Solidarność"

German Democratic Republic:
Stephan Bickhardt (theologian), Ibrahim M. Böhme, Martin Böttger (physicist), Bärbel Bohley (painter), Ulrike Constin (nurse), Uwe Dähn, Hansjürg Deschner (nurse), Reiner Dietrich (mechanic, member of the group "Peace and Human Rights"), Rainer Eppelmann (pastor), Irene Fechner (seamstress), Werner Fischer (illustrator), Steffen Gresch, Peter Grimm (industrial merchant, member of the group "Peace and Human Rights"), Sabine Grimm (nurse, member of the group "Peace and Human Rights"), Jens Gitzbrecht (mechanic), Martin Gutzeit, Monika Haeger, Ralf Hirsch (mechanic, member of the group "Peace and Human Rights"), Gerold Hildebrandt (nurse), Carlo Jordan (church employee), Jürgen Junghardt (mechanic), Uwe Kulisch (church employee), Heiko Lietz (theologian), Markus Meckel (pastor), Ludwig Mehlhorn (mathematician), Andrea Möller (salesperson, member of the group "Peace and Human Rights"), Olaf Möller (mechanic, "Peace and Human Rights"), Lutz Nagorski (teacher, member of the group "Peace and Human Rights"), Jens Oehmigen, Andreas Passarge (church employee), Gerd Poppe (physicist, member of the group "Peace and Human Rights"), Ulrike Poppe (member of the group „Peace and Human Rights"), Anne Quaßdorf (medical laboratory technician), Luth Rathenow (writer), Rüdiger Rosenthal (writer), Wolfgang Rüddenklau, Christian Schnippa, Sinico Schönfeld (computer technician), Helmut Stieler, Karin Teichert, Regina Templin, Wolfgang Templin (philosopher, member of the group "Peace and Human Rights"), Hans-Jochen Tschiche (chairperson of the Evangelical Academy, Magdeburg), Reinhard Weißhuhn, Mario Wetzky (construction worker)

Hungary:
Iván Bába (historian of literature), Gabriella Bartos (economist), Judith Biró (historian), Mátyás Biró (translator), Antal Bogád (postman), Rita Boronyák (librarian), György Dalos (writer), Gábor Demszky (sociologist), Gábor Dénes (filmmaker), Jószef Eliás (protestant clergyman), Sára Eliás (lawyer), Tibor Fényi (economist), György Fischer (sociologist and historian), Ferenc Hámori (grammar school teacher), Mikloś Haraszti (writer), András Hegedüs (sociologist and publicist, former politician), Agnes Herczeg (engineer), Iván Jávorszky (grammar school teacher), Enikö Jób (TV-editor), Gábor Kelemen (sociologist and engineer), János Kis (philosopher), Ferenc Köszeg (essayist), György Konrád (writer), László Kormos (engineer), András Kovacz (sociologist), László Kövér (jurist), Judith Krausz (teacher), Ferenc Langmár (economist), Julianna Mátrai (journalist), Ferenc Miszlivetz (sociologist and historian), Ferenc Molnár (economist), Katalin Molnár (economic researcher), András Nagy (grammar school teacher), Zsolt Nagy (historian), Zsolt Németh

(economist), Csilla Palotás (grammar school teacher), Tamás Perlaki (librarian), György Petri (writer), Tibor Philipp (translator), Lászlo Rajk (architect), Péter Sneé (film theorist), Miklós Sükösd (sociologist), Julia Szalai (sociologist), Pál Szalai (historian and publicist), Mihály Vajda (philosopher), Judit Varga (linguist), István Varró (teacher), Judit Vásárhelyi (librarian), László Vit (engineer)

Italy:
Giorgio Benvenuto (general secretary of the trade union UIL), Mario Colombo (secretary of the trade union CISL), Mario Dido (vice-president of the European Parliament – EP, Socialist Party – PSI), Roberto Formigoni (president of the political commission of the EP, Christian Democrat Party), Emilio Gabaglio (secretary of the trade union CISL), Wlodek Goldkorn (journalist), Ugo Intini (editor-in-chief of the newspaper "Avanti", MP for the PSI), Alexander Langer (journalist, member of the regional parliament for the "Alternative List for another South-Tyrol"), Jiři Pelikan (MEP for the PSI, Listy-group), Carlo Rippa di Meana (commissioner of the EEC in Brussels), Sergio Segre (president of the institutional commission of the EP, member of the central committee of the Communist Party – PCI), Valdo Spini (MP for the PSI, responsible for international relations), Enrico Testa (president of the "League for environment"), Carlo Tognoli (mayor of Milan, PSI), Alberto Tridente (trade unionist, MEP for Democrazia Proletaria) – Green List (Tuscany)

Netherlands:
Prof. Dr. Viro Beek (professor at the Technical University in Delft), Ria Beckers (chairwoman of the parliamentary fraction of the Radical Party, PPR), Herman Bode (former vice-president of the trade union FNV), W.J. Borgerhoff-Mülder (former president of the Amsterdam Court), Ina Brouwer (leading member of the Communist Party of the Netherlands), C. Commandeur (former member of the leadership of the trade union FNV), Marcel van Dam (director of the radio station VARA), Rudi van Dantzig (chief choreographer of the National Ballet), Dr. Ph. Everts (director of the Institute for International Studies Leiden), Dr. Mient Jan Faber (general secretary of the Inter-Church Peace Council – IKV), Prof. C. Flinterman (jurist at the University of Maastricht), Prof. J. de Graag (university lecturer on ethics), Ien van den Heuvel (MEP for the Social Democrat Party, PvdA), Simon Jelsma (media expert), Jan ter Laak (secretary of Pax Christi in the Netherlands), Prof. Dr. A. van Leeuwen sj., Sicco Mansholt (former chairperson of the EEC commission), Jan Minkiewicz (representative of the Polish group "Freedom and Peace" in the West), Sremco Mooi (general secretary of the Netherlands Reformed Church), Kees Nieuwerth (Quakers Netherlands), Alexander Pola (pianist and actor), Dr. W. Rood (ass. general secretary of the Roman-Catholic Church of the Netherlands), Herbart Ruitenberg (secretary of the initiative "Support Democratic Forces"), Dr. Rob Tielman (chairperson of the Humanists' Association of the Netherlands), Prof. Dr. Jan Tinbergen (economist), Prof. Dr. Hylke Tromp (peace researcher), Liesbeth den Uyl-van Vessen, J. van Veen (chairman of the organization "Church and World") – Bukovsky-Foundation (Amsterdam), Doverija Groep (Moscow Trust Support), VVDM (trade union for soldiers of the Netherlands)

Norway:

Dr. Sverre Dahl (translator), Erik Dammann (writer), Inge Eidsvaag (director of the Norwegian Humanist Academy), Trine Eklund (leading member of the Norwegian Peace Council), Otto Falkenberg (founding member of "amnesty international" in Norway), Björn Cato Funnemark (general secretary of the Norwegian Helsinki Committee), Prof. Dr. Johan Galtung (political scientist and peace researcher), Aleksander Gleichgewicht (deputy chairman of "Solidarity Norway-Poland"), Brigitte Grimstad (folk-singer, member of the initiative "Artists for Peace"), Victor Hellern (principal and writer), Theo Koritzinsky (leader of the Socialist Left Party, member of the Norwegian Parliament), Prof. Dr. Eva Nordland (chairwoman of the Norwegian Peace Society), Prof. Dr. Johan Vogt (economist, former president of the PEN-Club in Norway), Wieslaw Wika-Czarnowski (chairman of "Solidarity Norway-Poland")

Poland:

Marek Adamkiewicz (mathematician), Maciej Baranczyk (Freedom and Peace, Bydgoszcz), Wladyslaw Bartoszewski (historian, peace prize of the German booksellers 1986), Stanislaw Brodski (journalist), Leszek Budrewicz (writer), Jaroslaw Cieszynski (Freedom and Peace, Gdansk), Jacek Czaputowicz (economist, leading member of the group "Freedom and Peace"), Jaroslaw Dubiel (teacher), Slawomir Dutkiewicz (Freedom and Peace, Bydgoszcz), Wanda Falkowska (journalist), Krzysztof Galinski (Freedom and Peace, Sopot), Radoslaw Gawlik (Freedom and Peace, Wroclaw), Malgorzata Gorczewska (Freedom and Peace), Krzysztof Gotowicki (Freedom and Peace, Gdansk), Janusz Grzelak (psychologist, Warsaw University), Jaroslaw Guzy (sociologist), Agnieszka Guzy-Romaszewska (student), Andrzej Gwiazda (former member of the national leadership of Solidarność), Joanna Gwiazda-Duda (former member of the leadership of Soliarność in Gdansk), Boguslaw Gwozdz (Freedom and Peace, Gdynia), Stanislaw Handzlik (Solidarność-leader under martial law in Lenin Steelworks, Cracow), Hieronim Hodkiewicz, Agnieszka Holland (filmmaker), Piotr Ikonowicz (translator), Grzegorz Ilka (Freedom and Peace, Warsaw), Wladyslaw Jakowczyk (Freedom and Peace, Wroclaw), Henryk Jankowski (Catholic priest, Gdansk), Wojciech Jankowski (teacher), Aldona Jawlowska (sociologist at the Academy of Sciences, Warsaw), Krzysztof Jurski (Freedom and Peace, Szczecin), Anna Karska, Andrzej Kojder (sociologist at the University of Warsaw), Jerzy Kolarzowski (historian), Marek Kossakowski (journalist), Urszula Kowalska (Solidarność activist, Gdansk), Stanislaw Kowalski (Solidarność activist, Gdansk), Konrad Krementowski, Roland Kruk (geographer), Marek Krukowski (medical doctor), Wieslaw Kwiatkowski (Freedom and Peace, Gdynia), Wojciech Lamentowicz (sociologist at the University of Warsaw), Jan Jozef Lipski (historian of literature, former founding member of KOR and expert of Solidarność), Barbara Malak (psychologist at the University of Warsaw), Konstanty Miodowicz (ethnologist, former leading member of Solidarność), Andrzej Miszk (worker), Piotr Niemczyk (student, leading member of the group "Freedom and Peace"), Leszek Nowak (sociologist at the University of Poznan), Janusz Onyszkiewicz (mathematician, former spokesperson of Solidarność in Warsaw), Teresa Puchaczewska, Konstanty Radziwill (Freedom and Peace, Warsaw), Jan Maria Rokita (jurist), Zofia Romaszewska, Zbigniew Romaszewski (physicist, former founding member of KOR and leading activist of Solidarność), Bartlomiej Sienkiewicz (Freedom and Peace, Cracow), Krystyna Starczewska (sociologist at the Academy of Sciences, Warsaw), Stefan Starczewski (sociologist at the Academy of Sciences, Warsaw), Jacek Szymanderski (sociologist, former leading member of Solidarność), Jozef Teliga (chairperson of underground rural Solidarność), Jozef Tutow, Tomasz Wacko (historian), Anna Walentynowicz (worker, former leading member of Solidarność in Gdansk), Janusz Waluschko (Freedom and Peace, Gdansk), Dawid Warszawski (journalist, leading member of the Committee for Social Defense, KOS), Anna Wyka (sociologist at the Academy of Sciences, Warsaw), Gwido Zlatkes (writer), Tomasz Zmuda-Trzebiatowski (Freedom and Peace, Wejcherowo) – Freedom and Peace, KOS (Committee for Social Defense), Polish Helsinki Committee, Robotnik (political group and editorial board), ZON (Committee for Independent Teaching)

Spain:
Mariano Aguirre (collaborator of the Center for Peace Studies, Madrid), Teresa Angulo (councellor for the Spanish Ministry of Culture), Kepa Aulestia (general secretary of Euskadiko Ezkerra, member of the Spanish Parliament), Luis Eduardo Aute (composer and singer), Manuel Azcarate (journalist), Juan Maria Bandres (president of Euskadiko Ezkerra, member of the Spanish and the European Parliament), Manuel Bonmati (secretary for international affairs of the trade union UGT), Francisco Borges (collaborator of the "Foundation Largo Caballero"), Fernando Claudin (political scientist, director of the "Foundation Pablo Iglesias"), Maria José Gómara (general secretary of the Association for the United Nations), Enrique Gomariz (leading member of the peace organization MPDL, editor of the review "Tiempo de paz"), Maria Jesús Imaz (philosopher, collaborator of the "Foundation Largo Caballero"), Faustino Lastre (publisher), Federico Mañero (collaborator of the "Foundation Pablo Iglesias", former general secretary of the Socialist Youth), Miguel Angel Ordoñez (secretary of the trade union UGT), Manuel Ortuño (director of the Pablo-Iglesias-Publishers), Prof. Manuel Perez Ledesma (historian, University of Madrid), Marisa Rodriguez (leading member of the "Foundation Pablo Iglesias"), Francisca Sauquillo (senator of the Spanish Parliament for the PSOE, president of the peace organization MPDL), Carlos Trevilla (member of the leadership of the trade union UGT), Fernando Valenzuela (publicist and editor of the review "Letra Internacional"), Manuel Ventura (director of the "Foundation Largo Caballero"), José Maria Zufiaur (secretary of the trade union UGT, vice-president of the Economic Commission of the EEC)

Soviet Union:
"Group for the Establishment of Trust between the United States and the Soviet Union" in Moscow

Sweden:
Prof. Dr. Karl Birnbaum (scientific collaborator of the Swedish Institute for International Affairs), Hams Göran Franck (lawyer, MP for the Social Democrats), Christian Gerner (historian), Karina Hart (social worker), Zdeněk Hejzlar (journalist, Listy-group), Sven Lindquist (writer), Ingemar Simonsson (pastor), Ørjan Svedberg (art

256

historian), Bengt Thelin (chairperson of the National Board of Education), Sussane Westesson (architect)

Switzerland:
Prof. Richard Bäumlin (professor of constitutional law, MP for the Social Democrats), Dr. Hansjörg Braunschweig (MP for the Social Democrats), Angeline Fankhauser (MP for the Social Democrats), Anita Fetz (MP for the POCH), Max Frisch (writer), Susann Grogg-Poggli (Women for Peace, Berne), Pius Hafner (church councellor), Lukas Hartmann (writer), Prof. Dr. Arnold Künzli (philosopher), Prof. Dr. Jan Milic Lochmann (theologian), Prof. Dr. Markus Mattmüller (historian), Walter Reschler (MP for the Social Democrats, central secretary of the trade union VPOD), Jean Riesen (MP for the Social Democrats, delegate at the European Council), Prof. Dr. Jean Ziegler (writer, co-president of the International Committee of Social Scientists for Disarmament, International Cooperation and Peace) – Young Socialists of Switzerland, Swiss Peace Council, Women for Peace (Basle)

United Kingdom:
Geoffrey Beck (honorary secretary of the East-West Relations Advisory Committee, British Council of Churches), Peter Cadogan (secretary East-West Peace People), Dr. April Carter (member of Alternative Defense Commission), Howard Clarke (War Resisters International), Michael Hair-Duke (bischop of St. Andrews), Geoffrey Hoon (member of European Parliament for the Labour Party), Mary Kaldor (economist and peace researcher, editor of END-Journal), Jan Kavan (director of Palach Press agency, vice-president East European Cultural Foundation), John Keane (sociologist, Polytechnic of Central London), Veronica Kelly (War Resisters International), Arthur Lipow (department of politics, Birkbeck College, University of London), Lord Mayhew (Liberal member of House of Lords), Peter Murphy (member of END), Harold Pinter (playwright), Michael Randle (War Resisters International, coordinator of Alternative Defense Commission), Dr. Paul Rogers (member of Alternative Defense Commission), Stuart Weir (editor of the review „New Socialist", Labour Party), Jane Williams (member of END), David Winnick (MP for the Labour Party), Nigel Young (peace researcher) – Furthermore there are the signatures of the following members of the School for Peace Studies at the Bradford University: David Cooper, Dr. Malcolm Dando, Robert Francis, Dawn Glazier, Anne Hall, Geoffrey Hunt, Douglas Lawrence, Patrick Litherland, Toshifumi Murakumi, Simon Polchar, Dr. Andrew Rigby, Robert Swindells, Sarah Unger, Rosie Wallwork, Patricia Waugh, Veronika Whitty, Dr. Tom Woodhouse

United States
Edward Asner (actor), Andrea Ayvazian (director of training, Peace Development Fund), Joan Baez (folk-singer, Humanitas International), Gail Daneker (associate director of Campaign for Peace and Democracy, East/West), Richard Deats (US-USSR Reconciliation), Matthew Evangelista (University of Michigan, member of the working group for Alternative Defense), Melinda Fine (Nuclear Weapons Freeze Campaign), Cathy Fitzpatrick (Helsinki Watch), Randall Forsberg (director, Institute for Defense and Disarmament Studies, a founder of the Nuclear Weapons Freeze

Campaign), Margaret Gage (executive director of Peace Development Fund), Allen Ginsberg (poet and scholar), Tom Harrison (Campaign for Peace and Democracy, East/West), Adam Hochschild (editor of Mother Jones), Winton Jackson (editor of Across Frontiers), Michael Klare (director of the Five Colleges Peace and World Security Studies, Hampshire College), Joanne Landy (co-director of Campaign for Peace and Democracy, East/West), Bob McGlynn (Moscow-Trust Support Group), Pam Solo (co-director of Institute for Peace and International Security, a founder of the Nuclear Weapons Freeze Campaign), Beverly Woodward (coordinator, International Seminars on Training for Nonviolent Action) – Peace Activists East and West (Amherst, Massachusetts)

Yugoslavia:
Milan Apih (publicist), Alenka Arko (student, "People for Peace Culture", Ljubljana), Ingrid Bakše (peace activist, "People for Peace Culture", Ljubljana), Vladimir Dedijer (historian, former president of the Russell-Tribunals), Mojca Drča Murko (jurist and journalist), Pavle Gantar (sociologist, Ljubljana University), Zagorka Golubović (sociologist, University Belgrad), Niko Grafenauer (writer, editor of the review „Nova Revija"), Vekoslav Grmič (bishop), Marko Hren (mathematician, "People for Peace Culture", Ljubljana University), Spomenka Hribar (sociologist and pubicist, Ljubljana University), Tine Hribar (philosopher, Ljubljana), Drago Jančar (writer), Ivan Janković (jurist and publicist, member of the Committee for Protection of Thought, Belgrade), Janez Janša (journalist, defense expert), Manca Košir (communicologist, Ljubljana University), Matevž Krivic (jurist, Ljubljana University), Miran Lesjak (student, editing staff of the review "Katedra"), Tomaž Mastnak (sociologist at the Slowenian Academy of Sciences), Silva Mežnarić (sociologist and journalist), Rastko Močnik (sociologist, Ljubljana University), Zoja Močnik (publicist), Mira Oklobdžija (writer), Mladen Petretič (ecologist), Rudi Rizman (sociologist, Ljubljana University), Dimitrij Rupel (sociologist and publicist), Slobodan Samardžić (political scientist at the Institute for International Labour Movement, Belgrade), Božidar Slapšak (archeologist, Ljubljana University), Svetlana Slapšak (classical philologist, chairperson of the Committee for the Protection of Artistic Freedom, Belgrade), Lazar Stojanović (filmmaker), Anton Stres (theologian), Alojzij Suštar (archbishop of Slovenia), Veno Taufer (writer), Vesna Teržan (editing staff of the Students' Radio, Ljubljana), Gregor Tomc (sociologist), Andrej Ule (philosopher and mathematician, Ljubljana University), Mirjana Ule (psychologist, Ljubljana University), Ivan Vejvoda (political scientist, Institute for International Labour Movement, Belgrade), Slavoj Zižek (philosopher at the Institute of Sociology, Ljubljana)

(Please note that where organizations are given after a person's name, this is for identification purposes only.)

RESOURCES

The following organizations and publications regularly feature material on independent peace and environmental movements in Eastern Europe and the Soviet Union.

Across Frontiers
P.O. Box 2382
Berkeley, CA 94702
Quarterly journal.

ACT for Disarmament
456 Spadina Avenue
Toronto, Ontario M5T 2G8
Canada

Detente
c/o Anne Helgeson
Centre for Russian & East European Studies
University of Birmingham
P.O. Box 363
Birmingham, B15 2TT
England
Quarterly journal.

Die Grunen (Green Party)
Bundeshaus HT 718
D-5300 Bonn
Federal Republic of Germany

Disarmament Campaigns
P.O. Box 18747
2502 ES
The Hague
Netherlands

East European Reporter
East European Cultural Foundation
P.O. Box 222
London WC2H 9RP
England
Quarterly journal.

END Journal (European Nuclear Disarmament)
END
Southbank House, Black Prince Rd.
London SE1
England
Bi-monthly journal.

European Network for East-West Dialogue
c/o Dieter Esche
Niebuhrstr 61
1000 Berlin 12
Federal Republic of Germany
Regular bulletins.

Fellowship
Fellowship of Reconciliation
523 N. Broadway

Nyack, NY 10960
Monthly journal.

International Fellowship of Reconciliation
Hof Van Sonoy 17
1811 LD Alkmaar
The Netherlands
Journal. 5 times/yr.

International Peace Communication and Coordination Center
(IPCC)
P.O. Box 18747-2502 ES
The Hague
Netherlands

La Nouvelle Alternative
14-16, rue des Petits-Hotels
75010 Paris
France
Quarterly.

Labor Focus on Eastern Europe
c/o Crystal
46 Theobalds Road
London WC1 8NW
England
Three times/yr.

Listy
Vicolo della Guardiola 22

00186 Rome
Italy
Monthly bulletin.

On Gogol Boulevard
Neither East nor West
151 First Avenue #62
New York, NY 10003
Regular bulletin.

Osteuropa-Info
BucherPresse
Vertriebsgesellschaft
Postfach 500266
2000 Hamburg 50
Federal Republic of Germany
Quarterly.

Peace and Democracy News
Campaign for Peace and Democracy/East and West
P.O. Box 1640
Cathedral Station
New York, NY 10025
Newsletters and press releases.

Peace Magazine
Canadian Disarmament Information Service
736 Bathurst Street
Toronto, Ontario M5S 2R4
Canada

Bi-monthly.

Sojourners
Box 29272
Washington, DC 20017
Monthly journal.

MEMBERS AND STAFF

OF THE

U.S. HELSINKI WATCH COMMITTEE

Officers and Staff

Robert L. Bernstein, Chairman; Alice Henkin, Vice Chairman; Aryeh Neier, Vice Chairman; Jeri Laber, Executive Director; Catherine A. Fitzpatrick, Research Director; Susan Osnos, Press Director; Janet Fleischman, Program Coordinator; Holly J. Burkhalter, Washington Representative; Betsy Fee, Assistant to the Executive Director.

Members of the Committee

Roland Algrant, Christian Anfinsen, Millard Arnold, Lipman Bers, Hans A. Bethe, Charles Biblowit, Albert Bildner, Yvette Biro, Abraham Brumberg, Yvonne Braithwaite Burke, Sol C. Chaikin, Kenneth Clark, Roberta Cohen, Ellen Dahrendorf, Drew S. Days III, Istvan Deak, Robert Decatur, Adrian W. DeWind, E.L. Doctorow, Fr. Robert Drinan, Lee Elman, Stanley Engelstein, Jean Fairfax, Jonathan Fanton, Frances Farenthold, Alan R. Finberg, Bernard Fischman, Marvin E. Frankel, Donald M. Fraser, Ellen Futter, Charles H. Gabriel, Leonard Garment, Willard Gaylin, Bernard Gifford, John Glusman, Hanna Gray, Jack Greenberg, John Gutfreund, Rita Hauser, John Hersey, Elizabeth Holtzman, Lawrence Hughes, Susan Jacoby, Tamar

Jacoby, Anne Johnson, Philip M. Kaiser, Russell Karp, Stephen
Kass, Bentley Kassal, Marina Kaufman, Edward Kline, Winthrop
Knowlton, Margaret Lang, Norman Lear, Virginia Leary, Leon
Levy, Leon Lipson, Richard Maass, Elizabeth McCormack,
Robert McKay, Nancy Meiselas, Theodor Meron, Arthur Miller,
Toni Morrison, Daniel Nathans, Matthew Nimetz, Eleanor
Holmes Norton, John B. Oakes, Heinz R. Pagels, Bruce Rabb,
Andrzej Rapaczynski, Stuart Robinowitz, Felix G. Rohatyn,
William Schaufele, Donna E. Shalala, Stanley K. Sheinbaum,
Jerome Shestack, Sanford Solender, George Soros, Michael
Sovern, Svetlana Stone, Rose Styron, Jay Topkis, Liv Ullman,
Jorge Valls, Greg Wallance, Robert Penn Warren, Glenn Watts,
Susan Weber, Lois Whitman, Jerome Wiesner, Roger Wilkins.